The Complete
HAMBURGER

The Complete HAMBURGER

The History of America's Favorite Sandwich

Ronald L. McDonald

A Birch Lane Press Book
Published by Carol Publishing Group

A Birch Lane Press Book
Published by Carol Publishing Group
Birch Lane Press is a registered trademark of Carol Communications, Inc.

Neither this book nor the author have any connection to the McDonald's Corporation in Oak Brook, Illinois. The book was written without any assistance or encouragement from their present management. The opinions and observations expressed in this book are solely those of the author.

Editorial, sales and distribution, rights and permissions inquiries should be addressed to Carol Publishing Group, 120 Enterprise Avenue, Secaucus, N.J. 07094

In Canada: Canadian Manda Group, One Atlantic Avenue, Suite 105, Toronto, Ontario M6K 3E7

Carol Publishing books may be purchased in bulk at special discounts for sales promotion, fund-raising, or educational purposes. Special editions can be created to specifications. For details, contact Special Sales Department, 120 Enterprise Avenue, Secaucus, N.J. 07094.

Manufactured in the United States of America
10 9 8 7 6 5 4 3 2 1

Library of Congress Cataloging-in-Publication Data

McDonald, Ronald L.
    The complete hamburger : the history of America's favorite sandwich / Ronald L. McDonald.
       p.   cm.
    "A Birch Lane Press book."
    ISBN 1-55972-407-2
    1. Hamburgers. 2. Hamburgers—History. 3. McDonald's
Corporation. I. Title.
    TX749.5.B43M34   1997
    641.6'62—dc21   96-40491
                                                                           CIP

There are many people I would like to thank for their assistance with this book. I dedicate this book to Dorothy McDonald for the motivation, to Richard and Maurice McDonald for the inspiration, to Elly McDonald for her commitment and devotion. Thank you to Jane Rafal for her editing, to Carol Mann for her belief in the project, and to Hillel Black for his willingness to publish my first book.

Contents

McDonald's founder Richard J. McDonald, 1994.

Foreword by
Richard J. McDonald

The Founder of the McDonald's Restaurant Chain

Over the thirty-five years since my brother Maurice and I sold the McDonald's chain that we started and built, I have been asked the same questions by almost everyone. "Are you ever sorry you sold McDonald's?" and "Did you ever imagine McDonald's would be so big and popular?"

As simple as those questions sound, they really require complex answers. My brother Maurice and I never started out to be pioneers. We just wanted to build the best burger bar ever dreamed of, one that offered good food at the best value around. Today the standards we set are still upheld around the world.

In 1961 we sold the company that we had built from an idea into a nationally successful chain. We had started a new industry called franchising and we had reached our personal and financial goals. So, were we sorry we sold when we did? NO, not at all. And I don't believe that anyone then could ever have imagined that the name McDonald would become the most recognized restaurant trademark in the world.

I am glad you have had a chance to read Ronald's story of the beginnings of the McDonald brothers and the dream we worked to bring to life.

At eighty-six years old I have seen many things in my life, from the birth of silent movies to men walking on the moon, but I still feel proud when I see those "Golden Arches" that I designed and fought for. And I am proud of the smiles they bring to the fourth generation of children who still call McDonald's their favorite place to take their parents to eat.

Richard J. McDonald

Introduction

I'm not sure whether it was Rodney Dangerfield or some other great philosopher who first said "It's not easy being me," but whoever it was must have had me in mind. Over the years I have learned the truth of that very profound phrase.

I would think of it every time I was awakened at midnight or 1 A.M. by the incessant ringing of the telephone next to my bed. Usually it was someone I didn't know who wanted to talk about his experience with a "quarter pounder" or make some comment about the service he'd received at a McDonald's franchise restaurant.

Half asleep, I would try to be patient and explain that I, personally, had nothing to do with the operation of the restaurants that carry the name McDonald's, and that I was not a clown but a real person.

The response was invariably, "Then whom should I call?" or "Then why list your name in the phone book?"

Why was I having these conversations in the middle of the night? What did I owe these people? Finally, out of a desperate need for an uninterrupted night's sleep, I decided to keep the phone number of the McDonald's corporation in Oak Brook, Illinois, by the bed. When the calls came in, I could play telephone operator and dispense it. But sometimes a referral to the real offices of the McDonald's Corporation wasn't enough to appease some fry cook who was running late for work (a person who should know better than to call someone named Ronald McDonald in the first place). Or sometimes a customer just couldn't wait until the morning to share his brilliant suggestion for a new type of burger. Who did they think I was, Dave Thomas? Who knows, one of the people to whom I gave the Oak Brook number might have been that irate customer who spilled hot coffee in her lap!

After a few years of fighting this battle and trying to maintain my own identity, I opted for an unlisted phone number, and peace finally reigned. Things could change for the worse again if the same people who searched the phone book for the elusive Ronald McDonald decided to expand their searches on the World Wide Web, but at least they won't wake me up in the process.

The excitement in my everyday life didn't stop there, though. It is virtually impossible for me to make a restaurant reservation over the phone. Or do something as simple as order a pizza for delivery (even I can't eat hamburgers all the time). The guy on the other end of the line immediately assumes I'm really someone from his own company who is pulling his leg—and I never get my pizza delivered. Frankly, I have to admit that if my own secretary told me that Fred Flintstone or Yogi Bear had called for an appointment, I might be skeptical myself.

You see, there is virtually no place in the civilized world where the name Ronald McDonald doesn't mean hamburgers. And in many far-off places, the name Ronald McDonald seems to stand for America itself.

Over the years my own name has been the butt of hundreds of jokes, from people all around the world. "Hey Ron, is it really all beef and a quarter pound?" Or "You can tell it's Ronald when he sunbathes, he's the one with the sesame seed buns." Or "Where did they get the name Big Mac—or are you just bragging?" and so on and on. If I had just written them all down, by now I'd have enough material for a good stand-up comedy act.

People always say that they have conjured up a different image of how I should look, too. It's as if they expect me to be accompanied by a strange-looking character in prison garb who is trying to steal hamburgers all the time.

Actually, I have been very, very fortunate in real life and also in my business dealings. I have had the opportunity to travel to more than fifty countries on almost every continent in the world. I haven't made it to Australia or Antarctica yet, but there's still time. My name—whether listed as a visitor to the country or just on my American Express card at a hotel registration desk—has gotten me into some strange situations. Some of the experiences were pleasant, such as lunch with the president of Italy along with fifty or sixty other American businessmen representing companies such as GM, IBM, and Texas Instruments (although I never did understand what they were even talking about).

I've been invited to and enjoyed a dinner with Dr. Berisha, the president of Albania (after independence was won and capitalism had started), and a great lunch with Dr. Maxi, the prime minister. They even asked me to assist in opening a McDonald's in the capital city of Tirana. It seems they encountered McDonald's on their trips to the West and loved the hamburgers.

I've also been an honored guest of General Edyma, the president of Togo, a beautiful seacoast country in West Africa. And members of the Ruling Counsel in the People's Democratic Republic of Laos rolled out a threadbare red carpet for me in Vientienne, where they have real elephants walking around the streets.

The reaction I usually get from all these dignitaries and world leaders when they first meet me is one of disappointment. Maybe I don't fit their perceived image of what a person named Ronald McDonald should look like. After all, I don't have red hair—or really much hair on the top of my head at all, if the truth be known—and my shoe size is $8^{1}/_{2}$, not 25. At only five-foot-eight I look more like Richard Dreyfuss than the huge clown depicted in the TV ads.

Still, it is the hundreds of wonderful people I have had the opportunity to meet the world over that motivated me to write this book. Friends in such exotic places as Johannesburg, Tirana, and Karachi, to name a few, have encouraged me to write a book on hamburgers.

Why not? Hamburgers are one of my favorite subjects. If there was ever an award for the person who had eaten the greatest number and strangest varieties of hamburgers in the world, I would certainly win.

My digestive tract could be studied as a natural phenomenon by the Mayo Clinic, considering the amounts and types of meat it has processed over the years.

In almost all of the countries I've visited I have been given special recipes—sometimes dozens of them—by nice people who know that I collect hamburger recipes. Many of these recipes I have been fortunate enough to receive have been handed down from generation to generation to the present family members, and have now been passed to me, and I'm pleased to share them with you. Some have been given to me by the greatest chefs in the world. Each recipe reflects in a unique way what these people consider the great American standard food—the hamburger—prepared within their own cultural and cooking traditions.

I have also been fortunate—perhaps that isn't the best word; let's say honored—to be treated to hundreds of meals of these native versions served by my hosts. And although I can't say that all were enjoyable, each one was a new experience for my palate. As well as my eyes. Boy, you should have seen some of these concoctions. In one African visit the culinary delights included antelope and deer, which we ate under a fan so powerful that it blew away everything on the table, but without the fan we were at the mercy of huge, bottle-green flies that seemed to travel in groups of thousands.

In Asia, I had Buffalo meat with spices hot enough to remove chrome from a car bumper. I was never sure whether it was more uncomfortable on the way in or out, but it certainly was an experience. In Central America, a piglike animal called a tapir, with a smell so strong you couldn't breathe it and eat at the same time, was prepared with wild onions almost as strong as the meat. In Pakistan and Bangladesh, it was lamb and goat with marvelous seasonings. Here in North America I have eaten game such as bison, elk, moose, venison, wild turkey, and even alligator in burger form.

No matter how exotic the meat looked, or whether it was grilled over hardwoods I had never heard of, fried on a flat grill, baked in an earthen oven, or cooked in a pan, the aroma of the cooked ground meat always made my mouth water.

Vegetarians might not agree with my usual dietary choices, but I have also eaten a wide variety of all-vegetable "garden burgers" in my time. But in my opinion, anything other than 100 percent pure ground beef is exotic. (I can't let my friends in India hear me say that. They thought I was ignorant for eating what might once have been one of their relatives from a previous life.)

The bread for these sandwiches also varied tremendously from the standard round white bun I usually favor.

I've had hamburgers served on flat pita bread with the burger stuffed in the pocket in the middle. I've had soft, fluffy bread called nan that was wrapped around the meat like a blanket. And the coarse, heavy, cornmeal bread of West Africa that was cut into thick slices that were each twice the size of the burger. Still, no matter what they were, or what they called the sandwiches, they were all essentially hamburgers.

Personally, I'm a purist at heart when it comes to the toppings for my burger. My favorites are sweet onions (preferably Vidalias), grilled almost black, and French's old-fashioned yellow mustard, though I must admit to sometimes enjoying a change of pace with chutney or curry sauce and even a great Thai peanut sauce for a bit of zing. No matter what you call it or how you cook it or top it, a hamburger is still a hamburger and is the greatest food on earth.

For the past thirty years, I have spent hours explaining to the inquisitive how McDonald's was the original idea, concept, and success of two brilliant men named Richard (Dick) and Maurice (Mac) McDonald.

It is hard to explain to people who are familiar with the gigantic world leader in restaurants, McDonald's, that it really started as a small, one-stand hamburger bar run by two dedicated and talented brothers.

The unique design of the building with its "Golden Arches," the sign with the burger count on the bottom, the limited menu, and the concept that McDonald's is the favorite place kids take their parents to eat all were created fifty years ago by Richard and Maurice.

That was my second reason for writing this book about the hamburger: to try to show the path two hard-working and inventive men took to reach the American Dream.

As a young lad I spent countless hours with my grandmother Dorothy McDonald, who was a little over five feet tall and who weighed around a hundred pounds. To me, she towered over almost everyone around, and was truly a five-hundred-pound gorilla when it came to business. I was always hearing about the history of the great Scottish, Irish, and Welsh immigrants who came to America with nothing but dreams and went on to achieve great things that changed the world, or at least made it better for everyone.

These men with the same backgrounds as our family's became my heroes as I grew up. They included Andrew Carnegie, who built railroads and steel mills into a vast fortune and then built Carnegie Hall. There was Alexander Fleming, who discovered penicillin just in time to save Winston Churchill's life for the second time. (The first was as a child when Fleming saved a young Churchill from drowning.)

There was Alexander Graham Bell, whose telephone and other wonderful inventions have benefited all of mankind. And there was James Watt, whose steam engine probably did the most to change the world into what we see today.

But the greatest heroes I had in my heart were right here close to home, Richard and Mac, two men who have made the name McDonald known and respected around the world. These two men were not the first to make a hamburger, or even the first to design a chain that served hamburgers, but they were the first to gamble on that old American adage "If you build a better mousetrap the world will beat a path to your door."

These two men should be considered on the same level in history as Henry Ford or Harvey Firestone. The business they built employs more people than the Ford Motor Company and grosses more money than Firestone Tire and Rubber. Dick and Mac's concept has been exported to more countries than any other ever initiated in the United States, and has spread more good will and acceptance of American values than any of our diplomats dreamed of.

To me, these two men have achieved as much for America as has any industrialist in our modern history. Yet they aren't even mentioned as a footnote in most encyclopedias, or recognized for their talents and contributions to this country.

It is to them that I have dedicated this book. It was written with the deepest affection and the utmost respect for all the great pioneers who developed and continue to develop the hamburger into a symbol of America and of our robust desire to enjoy life.

Be sure to try some of my favorite burger recipes. They will let you experience the taste of hamburgers from around the world—without having to put up with all the hardships I did to get them. All of them are based on ground beef; who knows if you'll be able to find moose or buffalo at your local butcher.

And please remember, every time you eat a burger you are not just eating a meal, you are enjoying a true piece of history.

The Complete
HAMBURGER

The Burger, with fixings.

1

The Discovery of the Burger

I have found no place in the entire world where the word *hamburger* isn't recognized, regardless of the language being spoken. Most of the people I've met in the countries I've visited believe that the hamburger was probably an American invention. Our fast-food industry has expanded so far and so fast internationally that it has become synonymous with the hamburger sandwich.

Major chains such as McDonald's, Burger King, Wendy's, and Hardee's, to name just a few, have sprung up in every corner of the world. Continent after continent has been overtaken by an explosion of distinctive yellow-and-red buildings with American names and picturesque food symbols. In less than a century the hamburger has become the world's number-one restaurant item.

In countries and cultures where beef would never be considered for use in a sandwich, where the word *sandwich* itself was unknown in the local vocabulary, the hamburger has now become a diet staple.

Franchises from every established American chain have opened in far-off places such as Japan, Russia, Ukraine, Hungary, Poland, and even China. The hamburger has moved ahead and replaced traditional quick meals such as Japan's shark-meat hot dogs, which the Japanese eat at their baseball games. (I wonder if they also yell "Get your red hots" like we do.)

We have seen radical changes in the dining habits of Europeans that have been just as dramatic as the changes in their diets. In countries such as Austria, Switzerland, and Germany, the once popular wurst sandwiches, spicy sausages served in a French bread roll, didn't stand a chance against an all-American burger once it entered the market. Street vendors folded like houses of cards once the big American burgers appeared on the scene.

In the United States, the popularity of the hamburger on a bun has also risen tremendously since the end of World War I. The noble hot dog, once called "the American tube steak" by the great W. C. Fields, was at one time considered to be all of America's favorite sandwich, but no longer.

Nothing was ever considered more sacred and more American than mom's apple pie, but now even that has been equalled, if not replaced, by an all-meat patty on a sesame-seed bun. The 250 million individuals in our country consume an average of fifty pounds of meat per year. While that's not the highest per capita consumption of meat in the world, probably a bigger percentage of it is hamburgers than is the case anywhere else.

But who really invented this popular food?

Most experts on the origin of food and culture give formal credit for the invention of the hamburger to the Mongols, who centuries ago ate a ground-meat patty similar to the one we have today.

Beginning in the thirteenth century, the great "Golden Horde," an army of fierce horsemen that conquered everyone and every nation in its path, rolled across the steppes of Asia. From it emerged one of the world's most powerful conquerors, a man whose traditions in war, politics, and cooking were eventually carried around the world by his own men and the peoples he conquered. His name was Temujin, and the world referred to him as Genghis Khan. He and his offspring influenced the cultures of Asia and parts of Europe for centuries.

The Mongols were a fast-moving, cavalry-based army. Their men rode small, sturdy ponies and stayed in their saddles for long periods of time, sometimes days, without ever dismounting. They had little opportunity to stop and build a fire for their meals. In those days, the entire village would follow behind the mounted warriors on great wheeled carts they called "yurts," leading the army's huge herds of sheep, goats, oxen, and horses on their conquering trek.

The Mongol riders needed food that could be carried on their mounts and eaten easily with one hand while they rode. (Not unlike today's drivers, who eat an Egg McMuffin with one hand as they rush to the office in the morning while in control of 100-plus horses.)

Ground meat was the perfect choice for the Mongols. They could use scrapings of lamb of mutton, which were formed into flat patties. They placed these uncooked patties in rolled skins and carried them under their saddle until it was time to eat. The constant pressure mashed the meat between the saddle and the horse, tenderizing it as they rode.

In 1238, when Genghis Khan's descendant Kubla Khan invaded Moscow, the Mongols brought this unique and traditional dietary item with them. The Russians adopted it into their own cuisine with the name "steak Tartare," (Tartars being their name for the Mongols), though they were more fond of beef than the horsemeat, lamb, or goat that the Mongols preferred. Over the years, Russian chefs adapted and developed this new dish, refining it by adding chopped onions and raw eggs. It is still known today by its original name, made just as it was 750 years ago, and served in better restaurants all around the world.

The popularity of this new Russian delicacy spread quickly throughout Europe as sailors brought it with them to many different ports. But it was during the era of global expansion in the 1600s that today's true hamburger was born. In the seaport of Hamburg, Germany, a city-state that was becoming a major port of trade for all of Europe, the hamburger first assumed the name it carries today.

The Germans were known during that period as innovators in food and beverages. They readily took to this new food and adopted it as their own creation. The average German palate was not very excited by a bland food that was made up of raw ground meat, and German cooks soon supplied a more flavorful and Germanic touch. Small inns and food vendors all over the port started adding salt and pepper to the meat. Others mixed it with chopped onions, pickles, and even small sardines to give it a distinct flavor. Each vendor would try to outdo the competition by making a more distinctive creation.

Now, doesn't that sound like the antics of today's burger giants and their monthly new creations? At some point, though, an enterprising chef at a German *brauhaus* decided to cook the ground meat to see whether it would sell. No one knows if he did so because the meat was about to spoil or if he really intended to create a totally new dish for his patrons. All we do know is that the world started to consume this new food, and called it "the hamburger" after the town where it was developed.

In the United States, the Great Melting Pot, an enormous influx of immigrants from around the world began in the mid-nineteenth century. People by the tens of thousands were coming to America from Italy, Germany, Ireland, Poland, Russia, Holland, and the rest of Europe to find the streets of gold they had heard about. With them came the foods and cooking techniques from their homelands, foods that they adapted to the supplies of their new adopted country. The hamburger traveled particularly well because of its simplicity and the ease with which it could be prepared.

The burger that was imported from Germany was made in a way very similar to a dish already eaten by many Native American tribes. The Native Americans used buffalo and venison for their ground meat. They started by scraping the meat from the bones and skin as the Mongols had done, but then cooked the mound of scrapings on a flat rock in the center of an open fire.

Before there was fast food, there was quick lunch. "Hamburgs" topped the sandwich menu at this early-twentieth-century American restaurant.

Could it be that the hamburger really is American in origin after all?

In any case, the hamburger allowed these newly arrived Americans to use all the cheap scrap meat left over from the butcher's premium cuts. This permitted even the poorest of families to include meat in their diets. The toughest and oldest pieces of meat could be as tender and enjoyed with the same relish as the more expensive cuts of prime meats that better restaurants served to an elite clientele.

Because the meat used for this new food was a coarser grind than that used for traditional sausage, hamburger could be cooked and served without the necessity of stuffing it into a casing like the traditional German wurst, Polish kielbasa or

Scottish haggis. Instead the meat was formed into large, oval patties and served as hamburger beefsteak. Today that name is still used on menus around the world, and the dish itself is little changed from those early beginnings, except that its name has been shortened to hamburger steak.

In 1896, the dish received its first "official" recognition when it appeared in *Fanny Farmer's Boston Cooking School Cook Book*, at that time the housewives' bible on food preparation. From that point on, this new dish appeared on almost every

The Little Tavern, Louisville, 1928. This early burger joint urged customers to buy their hamburgers by the bag—echoing the newly minted (1921) White Castle restaurant slogan, "Buy 'em by the sack."

America, home of the hamburger.

restaurant menu on the Eastern seaboard. Since then, its popularity in America has never waned, even if it did undergo a temporary name change during World War I.

At that time, anything that was German or that had a German name was considered suspect and unpatriotic, so eating a food with a name that came from a German town was definitely an un-American act.

But the popularity of the dish illustrated the old saw that necessity is the mother of invention, and American restaurants pulled out the stops to save this popular dish—renaming the hamburger "Salisbury Steak." The food didn't change one iota, but to loyal Americans, eating something named after Dr. James Salisbury, a British nutrition expert, was much more palatable. Dr. Salisbury had extolled the virtues of the hamburger as a cure-all for many illnesses, allowing the food to be promoted on more than just flavor and taste. As soon as the war was over though, Dr. Salisbury's name slipped quickly into disuse and the good old hamburger regained its popular name.

There will undoubtedly be more changes in the way hamburger is prepared or served. I recently attended a National Restaurant Association show and saw a lot of new cooking apparatus: Contact cookers that cook a burger in ten seconds by passing electrical current directly through the meat, new kinds of grills that can prepare food as fast as you can order it. And just as the Russians changed the Mongol dish from lamb and goat to beef, the health-conscious are doing something similar today. In the markets we now find burgers made from ground turkey and chicken, and a few special selections made from textured soy protein. Manufacturers are trying hard to make an all-vegetable burger that tastes like the original beef.

But I suspect that no matter what new approach to cooking is developed or what exotic flavorings are added, our oldest fast food will remain basically the same. Hundreds of years from now people will still fire up the backyard grill and spend a Sunday afternoon enjoying charcoal-broiled, juicy hamburgers.

2

The Second American Revolution—The Rise and Rise of the Hamburger Industry

It was 1904 in America. The world had just rounded the corner of the twentieth century, and there seemed to be a new spirit of excitement moving all across the country. Fascinating new marvels were popping up all over. A man named Marconi had just successfully transmitted a telegraphic radio message from Cornwall in England to Newfoundland in North America, all the way across the Atlantic. Two brothers, Wilbur and Orville Wright, had just successfully flown in a motor-powered machine called an airplane, just like the birds. Small glass bulbs called electric lights were magically producing light from wires. A liquid called gasoline was used to power machines called automobiles that were replacing horses. And every day more new and miraculous inventions were breaking into the news. The Panama Canal, the most ambitious engineering project America ever undertook, was begun, and Teddy Roosevelt was elected president.

It was in this whirlwind of exciting events that an enterprising young grill cook became one of the first in the food industry to feel the stirrings of change. His name was Fletcher Davis, and he came from a little town called Athens in the state of Texas. The town was probably unknown to anyone from outside the state, and I'm sure most Texans hadn't heard of it either. Davis worked as a fry cook at a small local diner, but he had dreams, and he hoped that in this new atmosphere of change he, too, could figure out a way to make his fortune. Who could have known that this small-town cook would carry on a tradition started by the powerful Genghis Khan? Or that the spark that ignited an entire industry would be struck in little Athens, Texas?

One day while Davis was serving the regular patrons the same boring old blue-plate specials at the diner, he became inspired. He decided that, with a little modification, the hamburger steak he was serving with gravy and mashed potatoes might just make a great sandwich. So, much like the unknown German chef who decided that cooking the ground meat would improve its flavor, Davis—"Old Dave" as he was known to his friends—decided to see if he could improve on an already good idea.

First he pinched off a piece of the large raw hamburger steak and placed the small round patty of ground beef on his flat grill. He fried it until it was a crisp brown on both sides. It was smaller and thinner than the big hamburger steaks he was used to serving, and the shape was round instead of oblong, but the aroma of the cooked burger was just as tantalizing.

Then he placed the browned patty of meat between two thick slices of home-made Texas toast, a heavy white bread with a crisp, brown crust.

He added a thick slice of raw onion to the top and offered it as a special to his patrons to see if they would like it. Well, it didn't take long for word to spread that Old Dave had cooked up the best darn sandwich in Texas. It was so popular in Athens that when it was announced that the World's Fair would come to Saint

Louis, Missouri, Dave, at the urging of his friends and family, decided to gamble on his new sandwich and see if the rest of the country and the world would like it as much as the Texans had back home.

Davis opened up a concession stand that wasn't much more than a painted delivery wagon with a grill, and he started cooking up his round little patties of ground beef. The aroma of the hamburger sandwich wafted up and down the midway of the fair and aroused great interest in the visitors who followed this marvelous smell to the little stand. Soon there were people lining up to buy one of these tasty new Texas treats, all passing by the established vendors who were trying to compete with their hot dogs, chicken, ice cream, and other traditional snack foods.

The sensational hamburger sandwich that old Dave offered that summer spurred the growth of a new restaurant craze that raced across America and overseas.

In 1916, another enterprising young restaurant operator had watched with wonder the growth in popularity of this new hamburger sandwich. He decided that it wasn't just a fad, that this new concoction might just be here to stay. He saw that it was quickly overtaking the popular hot dog and seemed to be the food of choice for Americans at all socioeconomic levels.

Like Old Dave before him, and like many Americans after him, Walter Anderson just knew he could improve this sandwich to make it even better. After working with fresh ground beef for a while in different shapes, thicknesses, and cooking styles, he decided he could improve the flavor of the burger by flattening it out to an even thinner shape in a patty form.

This new-style burger could be cooked more quickly on both sides. When the grill was very hot, the meat could be seared, sealing in the natural juices and preventing it from becoming dry. Anderson had noticed that the thick patties he experimented with had to be cooked slowly on the grills at most diners. This was because the grills were also cooking eggs and other things, so their temperatures had to be kept lower. Anderson decided to use a special very hot grill just for hamburgers. Next, he decided that grilled onions would be better than raw ones, especially if they were grilled with the hamburger at the same time and on the same grill.

The next problem he had encountered with the hamburger sandwich of the day was that the slices of bread it was served on quickly soaked up the burger's juices and became soggy, so that the bread fell apart before a person could finish his meal. This meant that he couldn't prepare his burgers and place them on the bread in advance of the lunch rush. He needed to be fast enough at handing out these popular sandwiches to serve everyone during a lunch break. So he did something that no one else had ever done—he developed a bun specifically for the hamburger sandwich. The dough he selected was heavier than ordinary bread dough, and he formed it into small, square shapes that were just big enough for one of his new flat hamburgers.

The bun was then baked to a golden brown, giving it a denser crust on the top and bottom so the juices wouldn't soak through so quickly. This worked better than the slices of bread that had crusty sides. Walt's new bun also maintained a nice, soft center for the burger to sit on. After testing his creation, he found that this new bun would hold in the hamburger juices and the onions for a longer period without falling apart. The new burger was also neater, allowing the patron to take his time eating his meal, and tasted better on a bun than on the sandwich bread.

Walter Anderson was still working as a fry cook for someone else when he started to develop and test these revolutionary ideas, just as Davis had been in Texas. But his patrons gave his new sandwich such an overwhelmingly positive response that Walter just knew he had a real winner on his hands. In the best entrepreneurial spirit, he quit his job as a cook and used his life savings to purchase an old trolley car. His dream was to build a restaurant that featured his new burger on a bun as the main food item. He added five stools to the side of the trolley to create a lunch counter for the busy diner. Inside, he cleared out all the trolley seats and laid out a kitchen that was unique in its time. In fact, it was the forerunner of the fast-food restaurants we see today.

First Walt added a flat griddle that he had designed himself. The grill was a small, heavy, steel rectangular gas grill that could be heated up to 500 degrees F. (most grills cooked at 350 degrees). This was the forerunner of the commercial flat grills that are used today in most of the hamburger restaurants around the world.

Walt was in the food business before there were any regulations about the cleanliness of a restaurant or diner. He was well aware of why most diners were called "greasy spoons," and he had no intention of allowing his place to fall into that category. To show off the cleanliness of his restaurant, he broke tradition and placed his grill right up against the glass in the front of the trolley. This way people could tell that his restaurant was sanitary and clean before they ordered food from it because they could see him cooking right before their eyes. He was proved right: On his very first day of operation people lined up to watch Walt prepare these new burgers on a bun.

From his own experience living on a fry cook's wages, Anderson also understood that the average Joe had to watch his pennies. Anderson wanted his new sandwich to be affordable for everyone, so he kept his burger thin and the price at an affordable five cents. But to ensure that the food wasn't considered cheap just because the price was modest, he demanded that the meat and the buns be delivered fresh to the restaurant twice daily and made sure that his customers knew they were ordering the freshest sandwich in town.

By 1920, Anderson was operating a total of three hamburger stands in Wichita, Kansas, and he could see the potential grow even bigger. He decided it was time to seek out an investor to help him expand his young chain. The American dream was coming true for Walt, and he didn't want it to stop for lack of capital. He found a speculator who was much like himself, and he got the financial

E. W. "Billy" Ingram (pictured here) founded the White Castle restaurant chain with Walter Anderson.

backing of a real-estate investor named Edgar Waldo Ingram—Billy to his friends—and together they laid the foundation for a new, nationwide chain that survives today.

Since Billy was experienced in real estate, he wanted more than just another trolley operation. So they decided to design a distinctive-looking building that met all of Walt's requirements and also used Billy's real-estate talents.

Copycats of Walt's successful idea were springing up everywhere. Walt and Billy decided that they would make it more difficult to have one of these clones follow in their footsteps and make money from their success. Their new concept was inspired by the famous Water Tower in Chicago, a magnificent building that looked more like an American castle than an ordinary building.

They had special concrete blocks designed and cast to resemble castle stone, and they built the new building in a castle motif complete with towers and edge work. They painted the blocks a bright white to reflect on the outside the cleanliness Walt intended to maintain on the inside, and placed the new grills in the open again so that anyone coming in to eat could see that the food was being prepared in a clean and sanitary environment. They named their new chain "White Castle" after the building's design—and it maintains that name today.

Their concept of a small, affordable burger also caught on, and the five-cent hamburger entered the vernacular.

Soon all America wanted to buy a sack of the flavorful little burgers on a square bun with tasty grilled onions and a pickle, just as their motto exhorted.

A rendering of the Chicago Water Tower, the inspiration for the design of White Castle restaurants.

The first White Castle restaurant, Wichita, Kansas, 1921.

Anderson, now teamed up with an experienced investor, was able to grow and open more small stores. By 1921, they had four units in Wichita. By 1922, they had added two in El Dorado and three in Omaha, Nebraska. From there it was a veritable whirlwind of growth for the White Castle chain. By 1931, just ten short years after the two men teamed up, White Castle was operating 115 stores in Kansas, Nebraska, New Jersey, New York, Missouri, Minnesota, Michigan, Illinois, Kentucky, and Indiana.

An early advertisement for White Castle.

Walt and Billy also tried something new for their time: they began placing small advertisements in local newspapers to generate business. The ads trumpeted the five-cent price and included a picture of the building with the location address. In a short time, the rest of the restaurant industry followed suit and began advertising in print.

Within a matter of a few years dozens of copycats had adopted Walt and Billy's inventive ideas. Many of these later arrivals tried to pretend they *were* White Castle to capitalize on the chain's notoriety. Some even copied the name as closely as they could, identifying themselves as White Tower, White Diamond, White Manna, etc. Their buildings were also close clones, perhaps with different columns or a side entrance, but never deviating much from White Castle's clean white façade. Some of these later entrants are still in operation today. Krystal Burgers, for example, still operates more than 200 units. But the credit for America's first fast-food hamburger chain has to go to two very enterprising and inventive men, Anderson and Ingram.

Today we can see the continuation of their developments everywhere we look. Back in the 20s and 30s, employees were all adult men. Women were expected to stay home with the kids, and young people got allowances for chores, not jobs. The men were required to dress in spotless white uniforms at all times and be clean and neatly shaven to project a sanitary image.

The adjustable, disposable, sanitary white paper hat designed by White Castle founder Walter Anderson is still in use in kitchens around the world.

To avoid the problem of employees' hair falling onto the grill or burgers, Anderson designed an adjustable white paper hat that could be worn and thrown away when dirty. The uniforms came in small, medium, and large, but heads had a wide range of sizes. This disposable sanitary cap was practical because it would fit anyone and was cheap enough to be thrown away when it was stained with sweat or grease. Today we find it still in use in kitchens all over the world, little changed from Anderson's first design.

Billy Ingram, who was actively involved in the food part of the business, became a food industry pioneer by developing frozen, portion-controlled meat patties. This innovation was a departure from their original philosophy of using all fresh ingredients, but frozen patties were more sanitary than fresh meat that offered germs a place to grow, and freezing improved the consistency of the patties. They soon found that the frozen burgers actually maintained moisture better than fresh meat did when cooked on the hot grill, with no loss of flavor. Portion control also meant better cost control, and with the frozen patties they had less waste as the burgers didn't fall apart as they cooked.

By 1956, White Castle had served almost 100 million hamburgers, more than any other chain in America. Given the population at that time, this was a tremendous feat.

The burgers continued to evolve, and the patties were soon made with small holes in the middle. This allowed them to cook even faster and shrink less. Less shrinkage helped the chain maintain low prices in the face of rising food costs without downsizing its burger. By the early 1960s, a typical White Castle could serve three thousand hamburgers per hour using its new high-speed cooking method.

By 1987, the popularity of these little burgers had created a demand so great that White Castle was shipping frozen hamburgers to grocery store chains around the country. Anyone could enjoy these great little burgers anytime, just by popping them into a microwave. And today frozen White Castle burgers can still be found at most local supermarkets.

Americans are always striving to be bigger and better, so it wasn't surprising that the burger stands would do the same, especially with the proliferation of the automobile. Now every family owned a car and could travel across town to their favorite restaurant. The neighborhood diner no longer had a captive audience.

White Castle microwaveable burgers are available today at supermarkets nationwide.

White Tower, Detroit, was one of the first White Castle copycats, 1930.

White Way Hamburgers, another White Castle copycat, 1940.

Enter the new idea of a "drive-in" restaurant. Again it was a wily Texan who realized that many people were "just too darn lazy to git out of their cars to eat." So in 1921 J. O. Kirby opened America's first official drive-in restaurant in Dallas, Texas. He called it the "Pig Stand," a name only a Texan could love.

By 1927, there were twenty Pig Stand drive-in restaurants in locations stretching from Texas to California. These restaurants were nothing more than small, free-standing buildings equipped with flat grills and refrigerators, sitting in the middle of large vacant parking lots. The servers (still all men) wore starched white uniforms and white paper hats. They would walk to the automobiles and take the orders, walk back to the stand and place the order, then leave to take another order or deliver a previous order that was ready. The patrons sat safely in their cars and ate their meals from special trays that hung on the car door. It was quick and convenient, a relaxed way for the entire family to dine out.

Once again the imitators started generating clones. Each new chain wanted to be just like the originals—but improved enough to be more efficient and more

The White House Shop chain borrowed White Castle's slogan, too. This is Shop Number 2, 1951.

profitable. In some cases this was achieved by adding faster service, so that people would eat and leave and new patrons could take their place. Female carhops were hired to replace male servers, to attract traveling men and delivery people as well as families. Many of the carhops started wearing roller skates so they could take the orders and deliver the hot food even faster than they could by walking. Skating was also a lot more showy than a simple shuffle back and forth across the pavement.

Some chains added a special two-way speaker system to their operations. The kitchen would receive the order directly from the customer, eliminating many mistakes and speeding up the time it took for the carhops to deliver the orders to the cars.

Many of the early chains that started out as drive-ins have continued to grow, though they dispensed with curb service in the 1970s. Steak & Shake, A&W, Shoney's, and many others are still in business, but no longer as traditional drive-ins. Others, such as Sonic, continue to perpetuate the drive-in tradition across America by building new units in the same style as their 50s predecessors.

As the country grew, automobiles got larger, airplanes carried more passengers, and restaurants tried to outdo each other in size. In 1937, Bob Wian decided to see if he could do for the trusty hamburger what Chevrolet had done for the auto: make it bigger.

White House Shop Number 5, offered drive-in service to those who "blinked lights," 1953.

He decided that if one patty was good, two would surely be great. Using two per sandwich would allow the burgers to grow in size without sacrificing any of the original seared-in flavor and without adding to the cooking and preparation time for a sandwich.

Wian worked at developing the "Big Boy" sandwich, a hamburger with two beef patties and a bun that was also taller and sliced into three pieces to keep each of the patties separate. He topped each patty with lettuce and tomato, and the result was a towering mound. The Big Boy was so huge that no one could bite through it in one bite, and Wian thought it would just be a big joke, kind of an advertising gimmick like the seventeen-layer cake or the yard-high sundae. But the response to this new super burger was tremendous, and within months the Big Boy was famous. People would line up outside, waiting to try the monster of all ham-

Robert C. Wian's first restaurant, the home of the Big Boy, Glendale, California, 1936.

burgers. By 1946, Wian decided to franchise his now famous creation. He signed agreements with Dave Frish in Cincinnati, who started Frish's Big Boy, and went on offering the two-patty combination in its traditional style. Wian also went on to license other operators around the country, starting regional chains such as Bobs, Kips, Shoney's, Manner's, Elias, VIP's, JB's, Abdow's and Elby's, all under the "Big Boy" banner and all using as a logo the familiar chubby youngster in checkered pants eating a Big Boy sandwich. Big Boy restaurants soon covered the entire coun-

The original Big Boy logo, 1937.   The Big Boy logo as of 1988.

try and are still operating successfully today. All still feature the famous sandwich on their menu.

By the 1950s, the hamburger was more than just a food item; it was a symbol of America itself. Drive-ins were growing and flourishing, and they soon became meccas for young people, who adopted them as their hangouts. The drive-in was featured in virtually every teen movie that came out at that time, which glamorized them even more. Hollywood created a mystique that made drive-ins the only place to eat for the teenage crowd.

It was during this period of time that true legends were made and the new multinational corporations in the food industry were in their infancy. And it was during this period that two dynamic brothers started a new evolution that would carry the hamburger industry well beyond the confines of America's borders and into the hearts of the world itself.

These men were Richard and Maurice McDonald, and the chain they founded was called McDonald's.

3

Building Arches Out of Gold

I t was during the time of the Great Depression—a time when soup kitchens were the main source of food for many, and the entire world watched the painful slide of a great country into a nation of countless homeless and hungry people—that many of America's most enduring legends were born. One of the legends began when two young brothers of Irish-born parents decided to leave their home in Manchester, New Hampshire, and, just as Horace Greeley suggested, seek their fortune in California. Maurice and Richard McDonald had grown up in a warm and loving family environment that had taught them good values and the overriding virtues of honesty and hard work. Hard work was in fact the bedrock of their very lives, and they worked from the time they were old enough to understand the necessity for it.

Like many children of immigrant parents, they were encouraged to study hard and follow the examples set by other immigrants who had found their fortune on the streets of America. They read the accounts of Andrew Carnegie, a poor Scottish lad who stepped ashore at Ellis Island penniless and became one of the richest men in the world with nothing more than a belief in himself and a desire to succeed. They read of families such as the Kennedys, Rockefellers, Morgans, and others—all of whom made more than just money in America through their sweat and toil; they made a lasting mark on the world.

But though they had read about these men, the McDonald brothers never would have believed that they, too, would become fathers of an industry of global proportions, nor that their name would be as famous and well known as those of Ford and Edison. Certainly, they could never have believed that the name McDonald, more than any other name in this country, would come to represent the idea of America itself to the rest of the world.

Their father, a man of great pride but little formal education, believed that by working hard and being loyal to a single company he could provide for his family and his future at the same time. He had worked all of his adult life in a shoe factory trying to provide for the future security for his family.

He labored days, nights, and weekends, and managed to work his way through every department of the company during the years he was employed there, until he achieved a management position as plant foreman. Finally, after long years of hard work, his job provided sufficient money for the family and enough security so that the boys could continue to go to school.

Then came the most unexpected blow of his life. He lost his job during the Great Depression, and was devastated by the fact that decades of service meant nothing in the end but a pink slip and a cold handshake from the boss.

The young boys, Mac and Dick, witnessed this destruction of the man who had guided and nurtured them all their lives and vowed never to allow their own livelihood to depend on an employer.

It was then that they decided to "Go West Young Man to Seek Your Fortune." The two packed their meager belongings in a cardboard suitcase and started their long trek westward, leaving the only home they had ever known in New Hampshire and casting off the bitter memories of their father's pain. Upon arriving in the growing wonderland called California in the summer of 1928, twenty-five-year-old Maurice and eighteen-year-old Richard McDonald settled in the magical city of Hollywood.

No place on earth was as glamorous and exciting as Hollywood at the end of the 1920s. It was the home of movie stars and dreams, of real-life gangsters and that new wonder called the movies. Thinking that this might be the place where their future lay, the McDonald brothers applied themselves to jobs at Columbia Film Studios. They were right in the middle of the excitement and glamour of this new industry, but their jobs weren't glamorous at all—just hard work moving movie sets for the popular comedian, Ben Turpin, and driving trucks for the one-reel silent movie productions that were then the mainstay at the studio.

They knew the new movie industry had the potential to become gigantic, and they wanted to get in on the ground floor of that growth. So they started to save their money with the hope of one day owning a chain of movie theaters and showing the movies that they had helped make. It took them four years of struggle and sweat, but finally in 1933 they took a step toward their ultimate goal: They had enough money set aside to rent a movie theater, and had found one within their budget—an old vaudeville theater in Glendale, just outside Los Angeles, which they renamed the Beacon.

Their motto was "Let the Beacon guide you to better entertainment," and they gave 100 percent of their time and effort to make that so. But even with all their hard work and the many hours they put into it, the theater was only marginally successful. For four years they continued to work as hard as possible operating the theater and found that they never made any money on the movies themselves. The economy was in transition and people weren't spending the kind of money on entertainment that the brothers had hoped for. The only profits they made were from their food concession, and they used much of that money to allow them to continue the movie operations.

But because the McDonald brothers worked for themselves, they gained valuable business experience. They also remained on the lookout for opportunities in other business enterprises. They saw the explosive growth of the newest craze called "drive-in" restaurants, which were sprouting up all over California. It seemed to the brothers that everyone in the state now owned a car, and that eating out was fast becoming a big part of the California lifestyle. They watched with great interest as small roadside buildings popped up, surrounded by big parking lots and serviced by men in uniform who took the orders and delivered the food without the patrons ever leaving their cars. There was a small hot dog stand near their Beacon theater, for example, owned by their good friend Walter Wiley, which did a brisk business serving nothing but hot dogs and milk shakes.

The brothers began to reconsider their disappointment about the fact that the only profits their theater was producing came from the snack food served at its food concession. They decided instead to draw on that food concession experience, and on the understanding they'd developed from long hours of hard work about how to serve customers, and switch from the theater business to something they knew would make money—the restaurant business. Closing their beloved theater forever in 1937, they gambled once again on their future and opened a tiny drive-in restaurant near Pasadena.

The new place wasn't grand by anyone's standards, just a small building with a dozen stools and a lot serviced by three carhops. Dick would operate the grill all day, cooking hot dogs and juicing oranges for fresh orange juice. Mac took the orders, delivered the food to the carhops when it was ready, and made the change. But though the restaurant was small, the McDonald brothers finally had a real success on their hands.

One of the things they understood about the food business early on was the value of freshness. In fact, the fresh orange juice they served at their drive-in was one of their first innovations. They had discovered a big Sunkist orange packing plant

Maurice and Richard McDonald outside their San Bernadino "hamburger bar," 1948.

right in their area that sent California oranges all over the country. After a number of visits to the plant they'd noticed that workers never bothered collecting all the oranges that fell to the ground after the pickers had gone through the rows. They made a deal with Sunkist management to purchase the fallen oranges for a few cents per dozen, and then made regular trips to the grove to collect the oranges. They were able to offer their customers grove-fresh oranges, squeezed right in front of them, to have with their hot dogs, and they made a tidy profit from their extra effort.

The hot dog stand was built in an octagonal shape with glass all around the sides, giving it a fishbowl look, and was nicely located on the road that led to the busy Santa Anita racetrack. For three years Dick and Mac concentrated all their efforts on working hard and on learning all they could about the food business. They would study other operations of all types and visit as many as they could, adopting good ideas that made sense for their own operation and continuing to improve it as they went along.

By 1940, they had noticed that the population growth of San Bernardino, a working-class area just outside of sprawling Los Angeles, was outpacing all of the surrounding areas, and that the area hadn't yet been inundated with the many drive-in chains that were starting to cover the arteries leading into and out of Los Angeles. Deciding that they could do more business if they moved their business, they purchased a new location forty miles from their first one at the corner of Fourteenth and E Streets. Richard, who had always been the one with an eye for new opportunity, also proposed to Mac that they keep their building, but redesign it by cutting it in half and expanding the kitchen area slightly. They then had this more efficient structure—one with just a little over six hundred square feet of working space, almost all of it kitchen—transported to their new location.

The building's shape was unusual for its time, with its slanting roof line and walls of glass, giving it a decidedly modern look despite the fact that it was really only an old building with a face-lift. The new stainless-steel exterior walls the brothers had insisted on also made a big impression, since that expensive but easy-to-clean material was usually seen only on the interiors of buildings, and then used only sparsely.

The McDonald brothers also used a radical new design that exposed the entire kitchen to the full view of the general public. They were always proud of the standards for cleanliness that they had imposed on their operation, and felt that if the patrons could see just how clean the kitchen was, they would feel better about the food they ate.

The new McDonald's Brothers Burger Bar Drive-In was an instant success, greater than its owners could have imagined. Their timing for the drive-in craze was perfect. They now had twenty carhops instead of three and a parking lot that could hold 125 cars. Those patrons without cars could sit at one of the several stools placed on the outside counter, and watch as the fry cooks worked in the spotless, stainless-steel kitchen preparing the twenty-five menu items that were being served. The San

The San Bernadino McDonald's, after the evolution of "McDonald's New Self-Service System."

Bernardino High School was only a short four blocks away, and instantly the restaurant became the chosen student hangout. The food was priced according to the competition, with hamburgers selling for thirty-five cents, and their signature items were their famous barbecue pork sandwich, and spareribs that were smoked in a real pit with hickory wood chips that the McDonalds had delivered from Arkansas.

Success did have a price, however: the restaurant required literally all of their attention. They divided the operations so that Mac would work the days and Dick nights, and every once in awhile they would cover for each other to allow for some free time away from the place. Also, after a while the business itself didn't offer any challenge to the boys; it was just a moneymaker. Certainly they had nothing to complain about on that score. The restaurant was consistently grossing over $200,000 per year, making the brothers among the most affluent residents of San Bernardino. Not that anyone in the community could tell that they were joining the ranks of the local movers and shakers—unless they saw the twenty-five-room colonial mansion the brothers bought just outside of town. This was a real American palace, with swimming pool and tennis court. To everyone who knew them, they were the same regular, hard-working guys they always were, cooking up quick meals and serving everyone with a big smile and a friendly word.

But having been raised on a work ethic that made them feel they needed to constantly improve whatever they did, they didn't feel fulfilled just resting on their laurels. One thing Richard noticed was that whenever another drive-in opened, it always started out catering to a family trade. But as soon as the teenage kids began to use it as a local hangout, the families stopped coming and the business declined.

It was also becoming more difficult to deal with the high carhop turnover rate. Each new operation that moved into the area would offer higher wages to attract the more experienced carhops, driving the McDonalds' labor costs up to unmanageable proportions and making it harder to find and keep good, dependable employees. The same was true with their fry cooks. At their best, the fry cooks were a difficult group to keep employed and trained. The high heat of most kitchens and the smell of cooking grease meant a constant turnover. But in a market where wages were in an escalating spiral and qualified cooks were at a premium, they were even more difficult to find and hold.

The high costs of constantly replacing cutlery and glassware also attracted Richard's attention. The teenagers who were the main customers of the drive-ins would constantly take the utensils and milkshake glasses with them when they left, and the cost of replacements ate into profits. Bothered by all these details, the McDonald brothers decided that there must be a better way to operate, and that they were just the guys to find it. Their drive-in was still the most popular and successful place in town, but they knew there were more changes on the horizon for the restaurant business, and this time they were determined to lead the way.

They planned to sell their successful operation in 1948 and take advantage of the goodwill and name they had developed. The place had paid for itself many times over; now was the time to capitalize on that success and to free themselves to design a totally new restaurant concept. They were committed to making their new business more efficient, to suit what they perceived as a new era for the restaurant trade in the 1950s to come. The end of World War II was bringing a new attitude to the country, and the customer base was maturing.

But just before the brothers completed the sale of their operation, they realized that it might be smarter to revamp their present operation instead of starting from scratch. Finding a good location was going to be difficult, and the current one had served them very well for many years. Why, then, should they just cast it aside?

They carefully studied all the old sales receipts for the previous three years of operations and selected only the items on the menu that made up the bulk of their income. This would allow them to operate with a very limited menu and increase the speed of the service on the items they offered. They even eliminated their prized barbecue pit, although it had been the main focus of their advertising and menu. Their research showed that it was not producing the volume of sales or profits they had expected. To their surprise, they discovered that the most popular and profitable item on the entire menu was the hamburger.

Now armed with a firm idea of what direction to take, they started to work on ways to keep the food cost down and to pass the savings on to the customer. By making their new "Hamburger Bar," as they called it, the first self-service drive-up, instead of drive-in, they could pass on the savings of the cost of carhops to the patrons.

Next, they designed a system of equipment and procedures that would allow for speed in preparation, consistency of a high-quality product, low prices that were attractive to everybody, and high volume to justify all the efforts. Richard handled this project like a general planning a full-scale war. He covered every detail of kitchen operation and even counted the actual steps the employees would have to take to use the equipment.

He spent hours looking over all the restaurant equipment that was on the market, but couldn't find anything that came close to what he needed. Finally he decided to just go ahead and design what he needed himself and ignore the accepted industry standards. The next problem he faced was finding a food equipment supplier willing to manufacture these designs for a small, single-unit operation. Most were too busy with their own standard lines to assist a single operator, so he contacted a local one-man machine shop operated by a master craftsman named Edward Toman.

Toman had no experience at all in building commercial restaurant equipment, but after Richard took him on a tour of their operation he did understand exactly what Richard wanted to accomplish. Toman was caught up in the enthusiasm for the project and set to work in his shop with Richard's drawings.

Richard understood that the most important item for a high-volume operation would be sufficient grilling surface. He had spent enough time behind a grill to understand the need for speed. But the largest grills on the market at that time were only thirty-six inches long. Richard and Ed worked long hours coming up with a bigger-than-average grill that would meet his needs. He also worked with Ed to make heavier spatulas and scrapers than those on the market.

To be able to "dress" or add condiments to up to twenty-four hamburgers at one time, he designed a lazy susan that could be loaded with the bottoms of hamburger buns, then rolled over to the grill to receive the burgers. Then it was rolled back, the condiments were added, and the bun tops were put into place. None of this dressing operation interfered with the grill cooks, and by the time the burgers were wrapped, the next load was ready from the grill.

Richard also found that the traditional mustard and catsup dispensers available were inefficient for high-volume work. The dispensers couldn't be controlled enough to give a measured amount with a single squirt every time, and they didn't hold enough to keep up with the speed of the grill. With this in mind, Richard and Ed came up with their own design, a trigger dispenser that fired a consistent squirt with each depression and held a gallon of condiment. Now the burger dressers were able to rotate the lazy susan and cover the burgers in no time at all. Dick also realized that he needed a method to keep the food warm once it was prepared. For this he designed a heat bar that used calrods, metal bars that radiated almost 400 degrees of heat, as elements. None of this equipment was ever patented, but today it is still in use everywhere, and it has been adapted in a dozen ways by manufacturers around the world.

In 1948 the brothers closed the old McDonald's Drive-In and started a complete remodeling of their property. The carhops were let go and went to other drive-ins, and the windows that were used by carhops now became customer self-serve windows. The kitchen was completely remodeled and became unlike any other ever designed in the industry. Richard and Mac drew the kitchen layouts in chalk on the tennis court at their house, then walked back and forth to make sure that the equipment was placed just right for optimum performance and maximum efficiency. They even brought their cooks to the house and had them run through imaginary orders over and over. When the brothers were completely satisfied that they couldn't get it any better, they had an engineer incorporate the layout into the building design. The new kitchen had two six-foot-long flat grills of Richard's design, giving it more grilling area per square foot than any restaurant previously designed.

To eliminate the space and handling problems caused by cups and plates, the brothers designed a full line of disposable paper products for their menu items. And all foods that required the use of flatware were eliminated from the menu. With all the disposable items, there was now no need for a big dishwashing area or a big storage area, so the kitchen was lean and mean. To produce high volume, the employees were formed into teams, each charged with its own special area of responsibility.

Now came the real challenge for Dick and Mac—to come up with a totally new building design that was functional, attractive, and practical for the additional units they planned to open. Because by now it was obvious that they were going to expand the restaurant business into a chain, just as they had hoped to expand the theater business.

Richard wanted a building that was so distinctive that whenever people saw it they would know right away that it was a McDonald's hamburger stand. He sat down at his desk and drew the basic idea of fitting the building around the equipment needs of the kitchen, instead of making the equipment fit the building, but he still wasn't pleased. He wanted his building to be absolutely unique, different from anything else ever tried. He gave the restaurant a slanted roof in the front for the appearance of height. Then he added two large arches that rose high above the roof and resembled the letter *m* when seen from a distance, and he knew he finally had his design. His next job was trying to find an architect to do the final drawings for him.

But each one he met with saw the design and complained about the high arches on the building. Each one tried to convince Richard to stay with the traditional squatty building designs used by other operators. Finally he met with Stanley Meston of Fontana, California, who agreed to design the building just as Richard wanted—but without the arches. Richard was also working closely with George Dexter, a neon sign designer, and asked him to build the arches out of neon so that they could be seen from a great distance.

When Dexter was finished, Richard took the sign drawings back to Meston and insisted that they be incorporated into the overall design just as he wanted. To ensure a clean look for the exterior, they decided to have the building covered in shiny ceramic tile. This also added to the building's visibility and allowed it to be kept clean without constant repainting.

McDonald's in the Ray Kroc era. The McDonald's Corporation calls this the "original McDonald's.

The most striking area of change by far was in the menu they came up with and its policy of pricing lower than ever for a drive-in restaurant. The new offerings included a hamburger, a cheeseburger, three flavors of soft drinks all served in one size paper cup, milk, coffee, potato chips and pie. Given the limited choice of food items at the new restaurant, pricing had to be low enough to attract diners to this new self-serve concept. So the brothers cut the burger size from eight patties to the pound of ground beef to ten patties to the pound. And they had all the burgers prepared the same way, with mustard, onions, two pickle slices, and catsup. Then they

The menu at Ray Kroc's original franchise, which he called "McDonald's Number 1,"
c. 1955.

slashed the price from thirty-five cents each, which was the average price for a burger everywhere else, to an unbelievable fifteen cents, sending shock waves through the local competition.

Once they opened to the public, the McDonalds continued to work hard to streamline their techniques of preparation and service. Their team crews were like professional ball teams, and the brothers were the coaches, working on drills over and over until each member of the team could do his job blindfolded, as well as the jobs of the other team members. They advertised their new "Speedy System" and initiated the character "Speedy," a big hamburger with a smiling face and a chef's hat.

But the new restaurant wasn't the big hit the brothers had expected. Patrons would still park their cars in front of the building, blowing their horns for curb service that would never appear. Even the laid-off carhops and teenagers who used to come to the old place would stand around and heckle the workers, asking when they'd go back to the old drive-in system again.

The brothers never lost faith in their new concept of self-service. Instead they worked harder on improving the menu. They added milkshakes and replaced the potato chips with fresh-cut french fries. Within six months, business was back up to the dollar levels it had been before they closed, but with a new type of customer and a much lower cost. No longer a teenage hangout, the new self-serve restaurant was serving entire families, who could now afford to dine out with their children. The fishbowl design of the building was also a big help: The adults could see for themselves that the food was prepared in a clean kitchen with shiny stainless-steel equipment.

Self-service also became an exciting new attraction for the younger kids, who could approach the window and order for themselves while still keeping their parents safely in sight in the car. This new freedom for children made McDonald's what it still is today, the most popular place for children to take their parents to eat.

Richard's rigid training program of specialists in each area of the kitchen paid off in speed and efficiency. The "Grill Man" did nothing but cook the burgers and manage the patties and the grill; the "Shake Man" concentrated only on filling sodas and making milkshakes; and the "Fry Man" processed the french fries and operated the deep fryer. In the staging areas were the "Dressers," who dressed the burgers with ketchup, mustard, onion, and pickles, then wrapped them and placed them under heat lamps to keep them warm. The "Counter Men" served the customers as they came to the windows and made the change. Each specialist learned his duties and tasks according to the specific procedures that Richard laid down and practiced with them continually. The McDonald brothers had just done for the restaurant business what Henry Ford had done for the automobile—created an assembly line.

Their rapid food delivery service, paper service, and low pricing helped McDonald's expand rapidly. By 1951, the small restaurant was turning out $277,000 per year in income. By the mid fifties, it was up to $350,000 per year with profits that other restaurants could only imagine. It wasn't that they grossed that much more than other restaurants, but that money came in with a minimum number of employees in a very small space and that it was built primarily on fifteen-cent hamburgers. Maurice and Richard knew they had hit upon a winning combination of speed, quality, and price. They knew they had a distinctly different building design that could handle a huge sales volume. And they knew that the copy cats would be making an appearance very soon.

Their building could not be easily cloned, though. This would allow them to keep their operation distinct for a while longer. Richard's tall arches and slanted roof became the trademark of McDonald's that remains today.

By 1953, the McDonald brothers' fame and success had attracted attention from around the country, and they decided it was time to license their "Speedy

System" to other operators. The first license was sold for $1,000 to a Phoenix developer, Neil Fox. What Richard and Mac had sold was the high-speed service system and menu controls, or so they thought at the time.

Fox called his restaurant McDonald's too, which surprised the brothers, since no one outside of Southern California was even aware of their restaurant. The first concern that Richard had was keeping the new license operations at the same high standards he had demanded.

So they moved forward with a full franchising package that gave them controls on quality and standards. Within two years they had franchised fifteen units and were receiving so many inquiries that they never had to promote their franchises. Everyone was fascinated with the new chain that offered a standard building design and quality food on a consistent basis. People were coming from all over the country to see this new goldmine with golden arches that had people lining up around the block to buy hamburgers.

The problem with the new franchising concept was that the brothers didn't like to travel far from home. They were happy in California and not at all interested in the rapid expansion of their restaurant if it involved long trips. When it came to franchises, Richard and Mac weren't very good salesmen. They repeatedly turned away people who were interested in franchising, and managed the territories in a haphazard way. They were so busy operating their own units that the pressure of constantly overseeing the franchisees was taking all the fun out of the business again.

The Carnation Corporation took notice of the high volume of milkshake mix that McDonald's used, and wanted to bankroll the expansion of the chain across the country. With such powerful financial assistance, the McDonald's company could have spread like wildfire across the nation. But the idea of spending all their time on the road, staying in motels, and finding and training managers and supervisors wasn't what the McDonald brothers wanted out of life. As it was, they didn't even have time to enjoy the profits they were making. So they decided to turn the franchise operations over to a professional salesman named William Tansey. This freed them to expand their own operations while still allowing the franchise operation to grow. Still, there were problems because the McDonalds didn't have time to get out and supervise all the franchises to ensure that each operation was as clean and efficient as it should be. After all, franchising was still a new area, and they were among the pioneers trying to find their way while running a booming business at the same time.

It was about this time that a food service salesman named Ray Kroc walked into the picture. Kroc marketed the multiheaded milkshake mixer machines McDonald's used in lieu of the single-headed machine used at most drugstore soda fountains. What Ray Kroc saw when he arrived to service the McDonald's account was a phenomenon. People were crowded around the self-serve windows in lines that wrapped around the building, with a new customer being serviced at the window about every fifteen seconds. Kroc wanted to be more than just a food service salesman; he wanted to be part of this new phenomenon. He spent a full day talking to the customers waiting on line, all of whom gave glowing testimonials on the quality of the food and the speed of the service. After a long conversation with Richard about the multimixers, Kroc flew back to Chicago and pondered all that he had seen.

The brothers were your typical nice guys, proud to show their operation to any restaurant operators who were interested. This proved to be expensive for them in the end, because many of these operators went on to start their own clones based on the information and tours that the brothers conducted.

Some big players were also starting to loosen their purse strings in the area of expansion of chains in the booming business of hamburger stands. James Collins, the president of Collins Foods, for example, was the largest Kentucky Fried Chicken and Sizzler Steak Houses franchisee. He visited Richard and Mac and was given the full tour, and was even told where they got their equipment.

Ray A. Kroc, Des Plaines, Illinois.

Collins passed on the information and eventually aided in the setup of a number of chains.

Kroc, motivated also by a decline in the traditional markets for his multimixers, contacted Richard about becoming the franchise agent for the chain. It

The first crew at Ray Kroc's Des Plaines, Illinois, McDonald's, c. 1964.

was obvious that a business like McDonald's could be started for as little as $70,000—including land, building, and equipment—and operated with a minimum number of employees. With sales in the range of $300,000 to $400,000 per year, the business would pay for itself quickly. Meanwhile, the first copycats

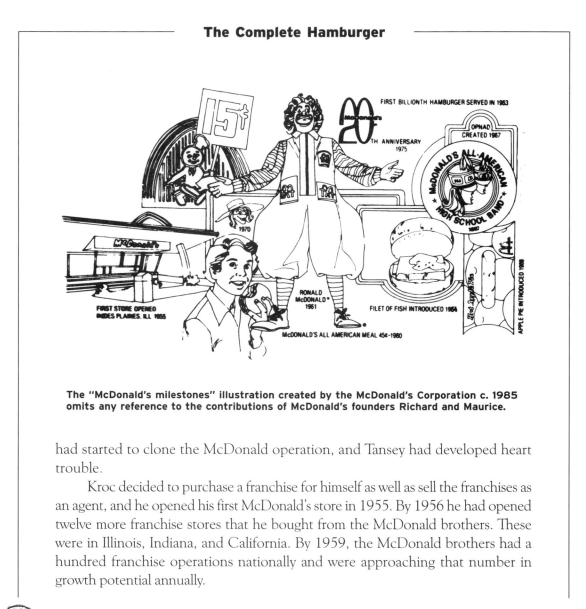

The "McDonald's milestones" illustration created by the McDonald's Corporation c. 1985 omits any reference to the contributions of McDonald's founders Richard and Maurice.

had started to clone the McDonald operation, and Tansey had developed heart trouble.

Kroc decided to purchase a franchise for himself as well as sell the franchises as an agent, and he opened his first McDonald's store in 1955. By 1956 he had opened twelve more franchise stores that he bought from the McDonald brothers. These were in Illinois, Indiana, and California. By 1959, the McDonald brothers had a hundred franchise operations nationally and were approaching that number in growth potential annually.

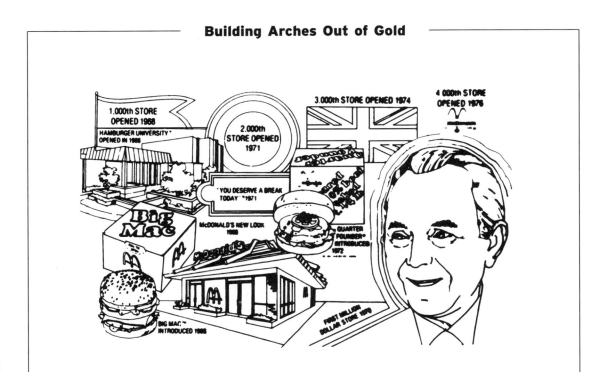

In 1961, seven years after Kroc had started working for and with the McDonald brothers, he decided to try to buy out the operation. His contract as exclusive franchise agent was running out, and buying the chain was the only way to ensure his continuation with the chain.

Meanwhile the brothers were ready to slow down and take it easier, so they agreed to sell the chain to Kroc for $2.7 million in cash. That year there were 228 operating McDonald's generating sales of $37.8 million. The McDonalds had achieved what their father always wanted: financial security. The sale of the chain would net Richard and Maurice $1 million each after taxes and they could slow down and enjoy the home in Palm Springs and the one in San Bernardino.

The rest is history. Today there are many companies that have been built on the principles that Maurice and Richard developed. These chains include Burger King, Wendy's, What A Burger, Hardee's, Burger Chef, Checkers, and dozens of others who have used the equipment, training, or techniques developed by the McDonald brothers.

So the next time you enter a McDonald's and see the golden arches welcoming you, remember it was the dream of two men named McDonald that made it possible.

4

Burger Wars

The incredible success of McDonald's quickly inspired a new generation of cloners—entrepreneurs who had learned from watching the successful expansion of chains like White Castle and Big Boy's. But these new followers riding on McDonald's coattails were far different from the restaurant operators of years past, who had hopes of building a single unit into a powerful chain. Now they were corporate types and money groups with better financing and bigger advertising budgets. No aspiring fry cooks here—these groups were made up of CPAs, attorneys, and bankers.

The bigger chains used advertising dollars to keep the competition from capturing too much of their territory, the same way military generals used troop buildups to restrain the enemy. These expenditures grew to the point where they are now in the hundreds of millions of dollars per year for each chain.

As each new chain opened up, it tried to keep its operations as close as possible to the original McDonald's concept, while attempting to add an innovative twist of its own to attract customers. Jack in the Box, a chain that is still in operation on the West Coast, used a new drive-through window concept to attract families who didn't want to get out of their cars to pick up their burgers. A clown head rising out of a box on a spring was its symbol, and the clown survives today. Since no good

The first Jack in the Box restaurant in San Diego, 1951.

idea goes uncopied, now every major chain is built with a drive-through window to service its customers. In fact, many new chains are built entirely around the drive-through concept, and some don't even have an eat-in area.

In 1952, a Florida drive-in operator named Keith Cramer decided to investigate the San Bernardino, California, McDonald's that had the entire restaurant industry in a tizzy. He watched in awe the business generated by this little hamburger

Jack in the Box was the first chain to offer "drive through" window service.

stand and decided that he wanted in on this newest dining craze. He met with the enterprising McDonald brothers, who gave him a tour of their operation, explaining to him every detail of their success. Cramer was sold, but he wanted something a little more unusual that he could start for himself in Florida. He visited an inventor in Hollywood named George Read, who had developed and patented a new machine he called the Insta-Burger Broiler. Read claimed that his machine could produce 450 burgers and toasted buns per hour with no chance for a mistake of overcooking.

When Cramer visited with Read and saw the machine in action he was fascinated by the concept. An experienced restaurant operator, he could appreciate the simplicity of placing a frozen, portion-controlled patty on a conveyor belt that carried it between two calrod heating elements that cooked it according to the speed of the conveyor. Using such a machine meant that you didn't need an experienced grill man to cook your burgers, only someone to load the machine. With one rod on top and one on the bottom, the patty traveled along its path and was cooked all the way through by the time it was deposited at the end of the belt and into a pan that contained warm liquid. At the same time, the buns were being toasted and dropped out the front of the machine into a separate pan ready for the patties and the condiments.

Cramer went back to Florida, and with the financial help of his stepfather purchased all the rights to Read's burger machine. Cramer took the machine to Jacksonville, where he opened the first Burger King restaurant. He was amazed that the new restaurant operation was able to sell over fifty thousand burgers at eighteen cents each in its first quarter of business operation. Cramer knew he had a good thing going, and he started down the path of franchising that McDonald's had already brought into fashion.

By 1956, there were forty-seven Burger King restaurants operating in twenty-two states, and the chain was growing rapidly. Burger King had adopted the image of a jolly-looking king seated on top of a big hamburger and mounted him atop a tower placed on the roof of each restaurant. In 1957, the chain had a sign designed that could be seen at night from a great distance. The king remained the same, but now he was neon and lights.

During this time of growth another entrant joined the McDonalds and entered into the burger wars. What-a-Burger decided to use the same flat grill system as did the McDonald brothers, but to make their burger wide and flat and to put it on an oversize bun. Popular right from the start, the What-a-Burger is still served in the same manner at What-a-Burger restaurants across America. Their building was also a takeoff on McDonald's distinctive golden arches, with a big W in place of the arches.

The original Jack in the Box logo.

Burger King's original Insta-Burger machines had started to show serious flaws once in production, and Dave Edgarton, a Miami franchisee of the chain, came up with a machine redesign. His idea used the same conveyor system but cooked with flames from natural gas instead of the electric calrods. He approached the Sani-Serve company, makers of ice cream machines, to manufacture these new broilers for the entire chain. His development remains today as Burger King's greatest claim to fame, the "Flame Broiled Hamburger".

Edgarton also copied What-a-Burger's wide flat burger and named it the "Whopper." Burger King started to market this bigger, four-and-a-half-inch bun with a four-ounce patty, adding all the trimmings to top it off. Priced at twenty-nine cents, it was more expensive than both their original burger and the competition, but it proved to be very popular. It also allowed Burger King to develop a catchy marketing phrase for that time, "It takes two hands to handle a Whopper."

Burger King continued to grow domestically and internationally and today operates more than seven thousand restaurants around the world. The word *Whopper* has become synonymous with the chain itself.

In 1958, the President of Sani-Serve decided that the burger business was just too good to pass up. He had been making the broiler for Burger King and business

Burger King ad, 1966.

seemed to grow by leaps and bounds, so why just make the equipment? He decided to enter the market himself and start his own chain. He started the Burger Chef chain by copying McDonald's systems and Burger King's equipment and basing the chain in Indianapolis, figuring that since Burger King was eating up the Southeast and McDonald's was devouring the West Coast, the Midwest would be virgin territory. His entree into the wars was a small double-decker cheeseburger called the "Big Chef." By the late 1960s, there were more than a thousand Burger Chef units operating all across the country.

Another enterprising restaurant operator named William Hardee decided that the Carolinas also needed a home-based chain to call their own. He, too, wanted to modify his burgers to be a little different from those of McDonald's, Burger King, What-a-Burger, and now Burger Chef. He opened up Hardee's in Greenville, North Carolina, and gave his burgers a distinctive outdoor flavor by broiling them over a charcoal flame instead of on a flat grill. The idea caught on, and soon Hardee's was also a household name in the growing franchise industry.

In 1972, Hardee's started to expand their operations by acquisition instead of just growth. It was obvious to Mr. Hardee that buying troubled chains was an inexpensive way to acquire valuable locations at a fraction of the cost to develop them, with the equipment thrown into the bargain for almost nothing. Hardee's bought Sandy's 255 units to add to their own, and became major players in the franchise race.

Hundreds of independent and smaller operations across America succumbed to the power of these major franchise chains. For a while it seemed that every day there was another new chain trying to tackle the multimillion-dollar advertising budgets of the majors, only to find that they couldn't compete. Carrol's, which had operated successfully in the East, realized that it was only a matter of time before they, too, were among the beaten, so they opted to have their entire chain become a Burger King franchise. A similar decision was made by the White Tower group.

What-A-Burger, San Antonio, 1983. The enclosed dining area in the front was originally an open, "drive-under" canopy.

After successfully copying White Castle, they found it easier to join a major national chain than to try to start over. So they also became Burger Kings.

The big food companies that had long been supplying these rapidly growing giants were watching as the numbers grew staggering. They decided that it was time to use some of those cash reserve positions they had to acquire the chains that they were serving and make sure they kept the supply side of the business.

In 1967, General Foods bought the Burger Chef group's six hundred restaurants for $15 million. Ralston Purina joined in the mania and purchased Jack in the

Box's 280 restaurants, and Pillsbury, not to be outdone, purchased the Burger King chain for $18 million.

No sane person would ever have thought of trying to enter into battle with these established burger giants at this time—but a new contender came on the scene to do exactly that. In 1969, a young millionaire named Dave Thomas—who had learned from one of the world's great success stories, Harlan Sanders, the venerable Colonel of fried chicken himself—decided to satisfy a dream that he'd had since he was a little boy.

Dave loved to eat and longed to return to the days when a hamburger was not just a frozen meat patty cooked dry and served with mustard, ketchup, and pickle. He wanted a real, old-fashioned hamburger that was juicy and fixed just the way he wanted it.

White Castle ad, c. 1996.

He named his new chain after his daughter, Wendy, and gave it an old-fashioned motif, dressing staff in candy-striped uniforms and caps reminiscent of those worn by turn-of-the-century newsboys. The restaurant interiors were designed to look more like an old-fashioned ice cream parlor, with imitation Tiffany lamps, than a modern burger shop, and, following the principles that had made other restaurant innovators great, he broke the rules.

Instead of trying to cook the hamburgers faster, Dave cooked them slower, so they would stay juicy. Instead of preassembling the burgers for quick delivery, his were created individually with exactly the condiments each customer wanted. He could boast that a customer had 256 options for different combinations for his burger at Wendy's. He eliminated the frozen meat patties and pressed each patty from fresh ground beef right at the restaurant. But that wasn't enough. Dave wanted to be totally different, so he developed a square patty—just as Walter Anderson had done six decades earlier.

Against all the odds, Dave Thomas managed to pull it off and make Wendy's a major force in the fast-food industry.

In 1982, the chains that had come to be known as the big three—McDonald's, Burger King, and Wendy's—were engaged in an all-out war. Burger King even ran TV and newspaper ads calling it the "Great American Hamburger War of 1982," and launched an $80 million ad campaign that assailed the frying techniques of McDonald's and Wendy's and touted the healthier method of flame broiling. The war caused lawsuits and heated charges of false and misleading advertising leveled by the other two. In an out-of-court settlement, the three agreed to cease their attacks on one another.

In 1984, the war heated up again. This time Wendy's took the field first by introducing into their television advertising campaign the grandma of all grandmas, Clara Peller. Over eighty years old and barely five feet tall, Ms. Peller stunned America by peering into a competitor's burger and asking querulously "Where's the beef?" The ad was aimed at Burger King's Whopper, and the three words "Where's the beef?" entered the American lexicon. The phrase was even used by then presidential candidate Walter Mondale, who questioned Gary Hart about his proposed programs by asking "Where's the beef, Gary?"

The campaign caused such a downturn in Whopper sales that Burger King changed the Whopper for the first time since its inception. The patty went from 3.6 ounces to 4.2 ounces and the bun got smaller. Burger King spent over $30 million on an ad campaign to tout this fact, though a few months later they quietly downsized the burger to 4 ounces from the 4.2 ounces they had advertised so heavily. When the powers-that-be at Hardee's discovered the secret burger

Wendy's, Bowling Green, Kentucky.

Jack in the Box "founder" Jack—the face of contemporary fast-food advertising.

shrinkage they went on the offensive, claiming that Burger King was trying to snow the public. Their ad showed a royal person using a magic wand to shrink a burger patty to a smaller size.

This advertising hardball took its toll on the remaining chains in the country. In 1982, Hardee's purchased the 650-unit Burger Chef chain; and in 1990 they bought Roy Rogers, giving Hardee's 4,022 units and moving them up to the level of the big three.

And just when you thought it was all over, and the chances for anyone to try to compete in the hamburger market seemed less than zero, the wars are heating up again. Checkers and Rally both recently developed a small two-window drive-through that offers a quarter-pound burger for ninety-nine cents all the time. They've been placing their units in shopping center parking lots, foregoing the expensive properties that the big four seem to fight over.

Once Checkers and Rally entered a market, McDonald's, Burger King, Wendy's, and Hardee's all came out with similarly priced menu items. And the major advertising budgets seemed to emphasize this price to knock out the little guy.

Well, we will just have to see what happens next. Only the future will tell us if this new breed of rapid drive-throughs will be able to survive, or whether we'll see a resurgence of innovative new contenders trying to do battle with the giants.

5

Outta'-This-World Burgers

In everyday life we accept the hamburger as just a good meal. It seems straightforward enough: a quarter pound of ground beef, give or take a few ounces, maybe some cheese on top, ketchup, mustard, perhaps some onion, and the whole thing served on a bun. What could be simpler? But there are some people around the world who have different ideas about what a burger should be. Once you read about some of these zany burgers, you'll never take your hamburgers for granted again.

The World's Biggest Burger

In little Seymour, Wisconsin, they know that size isn't everything, except maybe in burgers. On August 5, 1989, at the Ootagamie County Fair, they cooked up a burger that weighted 5,520 pounds and was twenty-one feet in diameter. Now, I don't know how big the bun was, but it sure must have been a record too.

World's Coldest Burger

In the tiny country of Bhutan located atop the Himalayan Mountains at over twenty-thousand feet above sea level is a small forty-room resort hotel called the

Druk. Located in the capital city of Thimphu, population about fifty thousand, its room service offers a steak tartare made from a high mountain goat. This has to be the coldest burger in the world and probably the coldest place in the world to eat a burger.

The World's Most Expensive Burger

The champion in the world of expensive beef comes from the town of Kobi in Japan. Here the steers are force-fed bottles of beer by attendants who constantly massage the beef as it is fed. When the beef is finally ready for market the steaks bring as much as $125 per pound, and the ground beef (I wouldn't dare call it hamburger at these prices) costs forty-five dollars per pound. It is definitely the most tender beef I have ever tasted.

The World's Hottest Burger

I once ate at a small place near the beautiful Sheraton Hotel in Bangkok, Thailand. Their burgers had the greatest aroma and carried a scent I wasn't familiar with. So I decided to have one and see if I could guess its seasonings. I took one bite and immediately had to down two Thai beers to quench the fire. When my translator quit laughing he told me that they season their burgers with a special hot pepper that grows only in Thailand. This has to be the world's hottest anything.

The World's Wildest Burger

Here is a treat that every gourmand must try at least once: a caribou burger. The hotel Metropole in Murmansk, Russia, doesn't have it on the menu but at customer request will arrange for one with a day or so notice. In Lapland caribou are used as we use cattle. The meat is sweet and rich with an indescribable flavor.

The World's Roundest Burger

For me, this contest ends in a tie between the oregano- and sage-flavored meatballs of Italy and the nutmeg and paprika flavors of Swedish meatballs. Both make a great sandwich, and since I couldn't choose between them I decided to list them both. You decide.

The World's Messiest Burger

This is also a difficult choice. In the United States honors go to the Sloppy Joe, cooked ground beef that is mixed with a tomato sauce and poured onto a bun. But Mexico has a burger called a Burrito that can be equally as messy. The difference is that it is served in a tortilla instead of on a bun.

The World's Strangest Burger Meats

Here is truly some "food for thought." Many countries have adapted meats traditionally used in their native cuisines to make tasty burger-type dishes. I have tried many of these myself and found each good in its own way.

Australia	Kangaroo
New Zealand	Emu (low in fat)
Africa	Antelope and Ostrich
Jordan	Camel hump
Honduras	Tapir (wild pig)
Japan	Shark
Aleutian Islands	Whale
Mongolia	Yak
Belgium	Horse
Finland	Reindeer

Vietnam	Water buffalo
Canada	Moose
United States	Bison
Texas (well, it's like a country)	Javelina (a peccary, or small wild pig)

I am sure I have overlooked some countries and some of the specialty meats that they use. As long as people enjoy burgers, we will continue to find exotic mixtures to grill and serve on a bun.

The World's Most Famous Burger Eaters

J. Wellington Wimpy   This famous pal of Popeye's did more for the reputation of the hamburger than has any other cartoon character. He often uttered the memorable line "I will gladly pay you Tuesday for a hamburger today."

Lyndon B. Johnson   The thirty-sixth president of the United States, once said that his White House chef made the best burgers anywhere. Chef Joe confessed he used ground-up thirty-five-dollar-per-pound aged sirloin.

Bill Clinton   This U.S. president has admitted to being a real burger aficionado and a great fan of the Big Mac.

Fonzie   My hero from the TV show "Happy Days" was always at Al's Diner enjoying a greasy burger.

The World's Best Movies About a Hamburger

Hamburger . . . The Motion Picture   A 1986 spoof on a place called Hamburger U., where budding new managers are trained in the art of Hamburgerology.

High Time (1960)   A movie about a hamburger mogul named Howard Harvey—played by Bing Crosby—who goes back to college at age fifty-one.

The World's Best TV Shows About a Hamburger

Saturday Night Live   Who could forget the Olympia Diner skits starring John Belushi as Pete the owner, and Dan Aykroyd as a cook? "Cheeseburger, cheese-burger, Pepsi, no Coke, chips."

You Can't Do That on Television   This long-running kids' show on Nickelodeon featured Barth's Burgery. Barth, played by Les Lye, was the only adult on the show. He was a cook, and a slob—unshaven, wearing a filthy apron and serving terrible food.

Perry Mason   Perry's archrival was none other than District Attorney Hamilton Burger, known as Ham Burger to his friends.

The World's Best Burger Slogan

Clara Peller said it best in Wendy's "Where's the Beef?" ad.

The World's Best Burger Song

The Steve Miller Band did a song called "Livin' in the USA." The most famous line from the song is "Somebody give me a cheeseburger!"

6

Born in the USA

The Best Burgers in America

Nobody says it better than one of my favorite artists, "The Boss" Bruce Springsteen in his song "Born in the USA": It's great to live in America. One of the things I enjoy most about our country is the enormous range of choice we have in everything, especially in the variety of places to dine out. Even though I have ordered and eaten thousands of burgers all over the country in almost every state, I wanted to try to do the impossible: compile a list of the top ten burgers in the country.

After months of research I realized that it was an impossible task. I was ending up with a few hundred ties for first place. To be fair, it was hard to compare just plain burgers. Each region of the country boasted a special type of burger that satisfied local tastes. And who am I to argue with their creations? So, to accomplish this monumental task I decided I needed help from other experts, rather than just relying on my own experiences. I wanted you to have the opinion and consensus of all of America.

I contacted the best-known food editors and gastronomes in all fifty of our United States. These professionals spend their time dining out and rating the restaurants in their areas. (Wouldn't you like that kind of job?) To add to their opinions, I consulted the results of polls their newspapers sometimes conduct to name the "Best Burger" in their town. Other events have included taste tests and cook-offs to determine who made the very best burgers in town.

Obviously this was a task that even Hercules would have found daunting, but with the help of these great people and their publications we were able to come down to a "Top Ten" list, with more than ninety pretty darn delicious runners-up, even though we could have made a Top Ten Thousand list and still been safe in directing you to a really Great Burger.

If you want to become a burger aficionado, try keeping notes about the places where you eat. Compare the freshness of the buns, meats, and fixings. Look for inventive and tasty new ways that a restaurant serves an old favorite. Every community of any size has some wonderful choices if you are just game enough to go out and try them. For now, we have done some of the work for you. To start you off on your quest for the best burgers in America, here are a few places you can try:

SOUTHWEST: DALLAS, TEXAS

The Point Restaurant

This is a personal addition to this list. I have enjoyed many a great burger at this traditional sports bar with pool tables and dart boards for entertainment. At lunch time it is standing room only as the place fills with a wide variety of people.

Executives in $500 suits are sitting next to the guys that clean their sewers and mow their grass. They all come for the three-quarter-pound burgers that are seasoned and grilled in a traditional Texas manner. The flavor of wood smoke goes all the way through, and the oversize patties are always juicy with the meat not too tightly pressed. You can't leave this Texas landmark hungry if you chow down on The Point's burger and an order of their fresh-cut french fries.

The Padre Grill, a classic American burger joint, 1940.

Nobody does beef like the Texans do, and after eighteen years of living in that wonderful state I can attest to that as an expert. And The Point always wins the People's Choice Award for its burgers.

NORTHWEST: PORTLAND, OREGON

Papa Hayden's Restaurant

Kyle O'Brien knows food. He is the Arts and Entertainment editor of the *Oregonian* in Portland. It seems that his readers are not shy when it comes to contributing their opinions about the best in the Northwest. The consistent vote for the restaurant that serves the greatest burgers in the Northwest is Papa Hayden's. Chef Chris Miller combines the freshest ground beef with his secret blend of spices and then chars the burgers to a crunchy brown over a real hardwood flame. To make sure that his burgers are a cut above, Chris tops them with aged Roquefort cheese and places them on a special fresh-baked boutique bun. And it is definitely better to go to Papa's than to try all that at home.

THE NORTHEAST: PORTLAND, MAINE

The Great Lost Bear

From the Northeast we have a special restaurant that offers a burger as original as its name and décor. This small local eatery has served burgers to some of America's best known personalities. I wouldn't be surprised if Portland's famous tale-spinner Stephen King has been inspired by the Great Lost Bear's famous burgers. I know that I have been inspired by nightmares when I eat them too late at night. Ray Routhier is a professional food editor and writes for the Maine *Telegram*. He has really seen it all in the Northeast when it comes to rough-and-tumble contests for the "best" category. For ten years the *Telegram* has encouraged its readers to stand up and vote with their taste buds and opinions. So if you think they can do only clam bakes in Maine, think again. In Portland, Maine, you can find a real prize-winning burger.

THE MIDWEST: CHICAGO, ILLINOIS

Peter Miller's Steak House, Evanston, tied with
Taylor Brewing Company, Naperville

With the help of Phil Vittel, the world-famous restaurant critic of the Chicago *Tribune*, we came up with a tie for the Midwest. Of course in Chicago there will always be at least two contenders. From Pete Miller's Steak house in Evanston comes a real steak burger. Here the chef uses fresh ground beef and mixes it with prime steak trimmings to create a real taste tantalizer with an indescribably pleasing texture. To complete this gourmet's delight, the burger is served on a fresh-baked crusty bun with a side of their famous plank fries and a tangy cole slaw flavored with just a hint of horseradish.

In the other corner of this contest is the Taylor Brewing Company in suburban Naperville. Here, besides great beer, they boast a ten-ounce burger advertised as extra lean (83 percent lean, so they say). The patrons of this little establishment enthusiastically support this savory concoction of a grilled burger topped with a unique mushroom-onion-and-wine-sauce glaze.

You will have to be the judge as two great eateries from an area that boasts some of the world's best restaurants compete for the title of the Best Burger in the Midwest.

Phil also added a special entrant in the veggie burger class, a category I shamelessly missed and Phil helped to remedy. His vote was for the Blind Faith Café in Evanston. This little oasis of health and nutrition offers a Blind Faith Burger that is a fresh mixture of tofu, oats, seeds, onions, carrots, fresh parsley and spices grilled golden brown. It is served on a whole-wheat bun (what else?). Well, it's not my choice for a bill o' fare, but I am sure for my vegetarian friends (even a carnivore like myself has a few) it is a great treat.

THE MID-ATLANTIC: ROANOKE, VIRGINIA

The Wolf Burger

In typical southern fashion Walter Rugaber, the publisher of the *Times World News*, sent his number-one restaurant critic on a quest to help me find the very best of the South in burgers. This turned up the Wolf Burger Restaurant, a small place that really classifies as a burger joint. Here they serve what Walt calls an "incomparable" example of a real American burger. Nothing fancy and no added frills, just good and meaty. The only concession to haute at the Wolf Burger is that their burger is served on a big English muffin (you can still see that early colonial influence here in Virginia) that catches all the rich juices and holds them in. So for a little southern charm and an old-fashioned favorite, stop by and give the Wolf a try.

THE ROCKIES: DENVER, COLORADO

Bistro Adde Brewster

The mountains of Colorado have more than just winter fun and great scenery. They also have one of America's top-ten hamburger spots. Larry Sutton, the publisher of the *Rocky Mountain News*, found us a real gem at Bistro Adde Brewster. Colorado boasts of being a real beef state, and here they show you that they live up to that boast, using real meat and plenty of it to make a burger a meal. You can't leave the Adde Brewster hungry if you order their Adde Burger. It will definitely leave you satisfied. So if you have made it to the Mile High city and want a Mile High treat give Adde Brewster a try. And tell Duey Kratzen, the manager, that Ron sent you.

THE BLUE RIDGE: HOT SPRINGS, ARKANSAS

Burgers and More . . .

In a city famous for its academic achievement, football, basketball, baseball, and horse racing, you might not expect to find one of the best burgers around. Burgers and More . . . seems to win every competition in this very competitive town when it comes to hamburgers. Here you can kick back and enjoy a good-sized patty of ground beef grilled to perfection and served your way. If you don't believe me, you can ask Penny Thornton of the *Sentinel-Record*. She has made the rounds of every burger place in town and agrees with the masses that Burgers and More . . . can't be beat in the Blue Ridge.

Lunch counter, 1942.

THE WEST: ALBUQUERQUE, NEW MEXICO

Dave's Not Here (Sante Fe) tied with
Outpost Bar and Grill (Carrizoz)

In New Mexico there is a dynamic duo for the Albuquerque *Journal* named
Fritz Thompson and Richard Pipes, who have covered the Southwest in a quest for

the best burgers around. These guys have literally eaten their way across the country, and they have found some of the most unique and flavorful burgers anywhere.

Dave's Not Here offers a special blend of spices that flavor their ground beef. They use a green chile topping made from a secret recipe that Chef Armando Rodriguez refuses to part with.

South of Albuquerque is a little town called Carrizoz. There, Faye Garcia owns the Outpost Bar & Grill and serves a gigantic burger that is big and juicy and covered in her own special New Mexico chili sauce. They do know how to cook in the Southwest.

So when traveling off the beaten path be sure to beat a path to these two gems; it's worth the travel time.

THE SOUTH: JACKSON, MISSISSIPPI

CS's Restaurant

Thanks to Epicurious, the mysterious and infamous restaurant critic of the *Clarion-Ledger* in Jackson, Mississippi, we have found not only the best burger place in the area but also a totally new burger for my McDonald Burger Archives. At CS's Restaurant they make the Inez Burger, eight ounces of ground beef grilled and topped with homemade chili and melted nacho cheese. The power brokers in Jackson wheel and deal while they chow down on this tasty meal. Ep also introduced me to a unique concoction found only in Mississippi, but which could become a trend all over. (Well, stranger things have happened, haven't they?) It is called the "Slugburger," and has nothing to do with the slimy creatures found on sidewalks after a rain but was named after the phony coins. The burger is enhanced with soymeal to give it extra bulk, then coated like a chicken-fried steak and deep fried. This local favorite can be found at a number of restaurants in the area. For the brave and adventurous it is a must try.

THE SOUTHEAST: NAPLES, FLORIDA

Cheeburger, Cheeburger

My nephew, Ryan Thomas, insisted that I include our Florida landmark burger joint and I had to agree. They do have an exceptional hamburger—all one full pound of it. That's right, sixteen ounces of ground beef on a great big bun. It is good and really big enough for four people. If you finish one, you get your name listed on the wall of fame. (I might add that Ryan's name and photo are there more than once.) This restaurant has burgers of regular size for those of us with lesser appetites, and the regular burgers are very, very good. So try more than just the sunshine and seafood when visiting Florida. We also take our burgers seriously.

THE PRETTY-DARN-DELICIOUS
TENTH-PLACE WINNERS

Author's Note: Where two restaurants are listed for the same city, the results were a tie.

ALABAMA
| Birmingham | *Johnny Rockets* | *Birmingham News*, JoEllen O'Hara |
| | *Back Yard Burgers* | |

ALASKA
| Anchorage | *Arctic Roadrunner* | *Anchorage Daily News*, Fuller Cowell |

ARIZONA
| Mesa | *Angel's* | *Mesa Tribune*, Carrie White |

ARKANSAS
| Little Rock | *Buffalo Grill* | *Democrat-Gazette*, Griffin Smith Jr. |
| Siloam Springs | *Barnette's Dairyette* | *Democrat*, Irene Wassal |

Scot	*Cotthams*	*Democrat*, Irene Wassal
Newport	*Money's*	*Times-Herald*, Tamara Johnson
	Poppy's	

CALIFORNIA
Bakersfield	*Burger Hut*	*Californian*, Staff consensus
	Bootleggers	
Marina Del Rey	*The Cheesecake Factory*	*Argonaut*, David Johnson
San Diego	*The Longhorn*	*San Diego Union*, Patricia Dibsey
San Francisco	*Balboa Café*	*Key* Magazine, Brian Stott
San Jose	*Original Joe's*	*Metro*, Karin in "Features"

CONNECTICUT
| New Haven | *Louie's* | *Register*, Rick Sandels |

DELAWARE
| Wilmington | *The Charcoal Pit* | *News Journal*, Valerie Helmbreck |

FLORIDA
| Key West | *Sloppy Joe's* | *Citizen*, Winston Burrell |

GEORGIA
| Atlanta | *The Vortex* | *Atlanta Constitution*, Staff consensus |

IDAHO
| Boise | *Players* | *Statesman*, John Anderson |

ILLINOIS
| Champaign | *Murphy's Pub* | *News-Gazette*, Staff consensus |
| Joliet | *Bubba's* | *Herald-News*, Staff consensus |

LeMont	*Nick's*	*Herald-News*, Staff consensus
Wilmington	*The Launching Pad*	*Herald-News*, Staff consensus

INDIANA
Bloomington	*Nick's English Hut*	*Herald Times*, Bryan Worth
Fort Wayne	*Heinecke's Lunch Box*	*Journal-Gazette*, Sandy Clark

IOWA
Davenport	*Boozie's*	*Quad City Times*, Readers' Choice

KANSAS
Kansas City	*Winstead's*	*Kansan*, Mary Rugert
Topeka	*Miami Tavern and Grill*	*Capital-Journal*, Mark Sumer
Wichita	*Oasis Lounge*	*Wichita Eagle*, Diane Lewis

KENTUCKY
Bowling Green	*Jessie's Deli*	*Daily News*, Dave Bower
Lexington	*Lyngahs*	*Around the Town*, Staff consensus

LOUISIANA
Baton Rouge	*Brewbacher's Grill*	*Advocate*, Tommy Simmons
Hammond	*Tony's Tavern*	*Advocate*, Tommy Simmons
Lafayette	*Buns* *Judice Inn*	*Daily Advertiser*, Judy Stanford
New Orleans	*Port of Call* *Mid City Grill*	*New Orleans Magazine*, Chris Masciere

MARYLAND
Baltimore	*McCabes*	*Baltimore Sun*, People's Choice

Born in the USA

MASSACHUSETTS
Boston — *The Burger Cottage* — *Boston Globe*, Editorial staff

MICHIGAN
Bay City — *O'Hare's* — *Bay City Times*, Patty Lalone
Muskegon — *The Station Grill* — *Muskegon Chronicle*, Mary Franklin
Lavonia — *The Stables Bar* — *Lavonia Observer*, Daryl Clem

MINNESOTA
Rochester — *The Smiling Moose* — *Post Bulletin*, Kathy Rasmussen

MISSISSIPPI
Hattiesburg — *Chesterfield's* — *Advertiser-News*, Linda McMurtrey
Columbia — *Jack's* — *Advertiser-News*, Linda McMurtrey

MISSOURI
Columbia — *Booche's* — *Daily Tribune*, Donna Pierce
St. Louis — *O'Connell's Club* — *Post Dispatch*, Judy Evans
University City — *Blueberry Hill* — *Post Dispatch*, Judy Evans

MONTANA
Billings — *Tiny's Tavern* — *Gazette*, Karen Vaughn
Butte — *Matt's Place* — *The Standard*, Carmen Winslow

NEBRASKA
Lincoln — *Grotto's* — *Journal-Star*, Missy Lowery

NEVADA
Las Vegas — *Oasis Bar and Grill Melrose Place* — *Review-Journal*, Rinell Botwunik

NEW HAMPSHIRE
  Manchester   *The Back Room*   *Union Leader*, Alan Jahn

NEW JERSEY
  Atlantic City   *The Flying Cloud Café*   *Atlantic City Press*, Cindy Nevitt
                   The Knife and Fork
  Camden   *American Grill*   *Courier Post*, Staff consensus

NEW YORK
  Albany   *Lexington Grill*   *The Times Union*, Staff consensus
            The Barnsider
  Buffalo   *Jimmy Mac's*   *Buffalo News*, Janice Okun
             The Place
  Brooklyn   *King's Plaza Diner*   *Bay Ridge Courier*, Staff consensus
  Manhattan   *Old Town Bar and Grill*   *New York Press*, Readers' Poll
  Syracuse   *Crown Bar and Grill*   *Post Standard*, Janet in "Features"

NORTH CAROLINA
  Asheville   *Burgermeister*   *Citizen-Times*, Carol Curry
               West Side Grill
  Durham   *Wimpy's*   *Herald-Sun*, Al Carson
  Raleigh   *Char Grill*   *Herald-Sun*, Al Carson
  Rocky Mount   *Booney's*   *Herald-Sun*, Al Carson
  Pineville   *Teddy's*   *Charlotte Observer*, Jerry Hostetler
  Charlotte   *South 21*   *Charlotte Observer*, Jerry Hostetler

NORTH DAKOTA
Fargo	*Old Broadway Bar and Grill*	*Fargo Forum*, Missy in "Features"
Grand Forks	*Riverside Grill*	*Grand Forks Herald*, Daryl Cooler

OHIO
Akron	*Louie's*	*Beacon Journal*, Readers' Poll
Canton	*Menches Brothers*	*Canton Repository*, Cathy Smith
Cleveland	*Heck's*	*Cleveland Plain Dealer*, John Long
	Pig Heaven	

OKLAHOMA
Oklahoma City	*Chili's*	*Oklahoman*, Editorial staff consensus
Tulsa	*Goldie's*	*Tulsa World*, Terrel Lester

OREGON
Portland	*Carnival*	*Oregonian*, Pete Byson
Salem	*Rockin' Rogers*	*Statesman Journal*, Readers' Poll

PENNSYLVANIA
Pittsburgh	*T'saros*	*Post Gazette*, Woodene Merriman
Scranton	*Shookey's*	*Scranton Times*, Terry Lyons
Philadelphia	*Nifty Fifty's*	*Inquirer*, People's Choice
	Charlie's	

SOUTH CAROLINA
Columbia	*Rockaway Athletic Club*	*The State*, Carol Ward
Greenville	*Fall Street Café*	*Greenville News*, Jimmy Cornelison
Spartanburg	*The Beacon*	Author's Choice

SOUTH DAKOTA
  Sioux Falls   *The Hamburger Shop*   *Argus Leader*, Consensus

TENNESSEE
  Knoxville   *Litton's*   *News Sentinel*, Louise Durman
  Memphis   *Huey's*   *Commercial Appeal*, Chris Gang

TEXAS
  Fort Worth   *Kincade's*   *Star Telegram*, Editorial staff
                                               consensus
  Houston   *Chili's*   *Chronicle*, Editorial staff consensus

UTAH
  Salt Lake City   *The Brewery*   *Salt Lake Tribune*, Editorial staff
                                               consensus
  Provo   *Reams Grocery*   *Daily Herald*, Nancy and Friends

VERMONT
  Burlington   *Daily Planet*   *Burlington Free Press*, Debbie Solomon

VIRGINIA
  Richmond   *Mayo's Place*   *Times Dispatch*, Jody Rathskef

WASHINGTON
  Seattle   *FX McCrory's Steak,* *Seattle Times*, John Hinterburger
                       Chop and Oyster
                       House
  Spokane   *The Ram Cafe*   *Spokesman Review*, Leslie Kelly

WEST VIRGINIA
  Huntington   *Jim's Steak and*   *Herald Dispatch*, Brenda Lucas
                       Spaghetti
  Charleston   *The Blossom*   *Daily Mail*, Bill Sohovich

WISCONSIN
    Madison   *Dottie Dumpling's*   *State Journal*, Brian Howell
    Milwaukee   *Erv's Mug*   *Journal/Sentinel*, consensus
                     Georgie Porgie's

WYOMING
    Casper   *The Branding Iron*   *Star Tribune*, Newsroom consensus
    Cheyenne   *Lexi's Grill*   *Tribune-Eagle*, Newsroom consensus

Well, we had thousands of places to choose from, and I apologize for not being able to list all of them. From all the input I do know that in almost every city in America there is at least one place that takes pride in serving an exceptional burger. There are also so many local varieties and specialty burgers that you could eat one a day for a lifetime and still not be able to consume one of each. What a great food the hamburger is, it has so many tastes but still remains the same. It is truly affordable for anyone. So whether you like the convenience of a quick drive through, an offering from a major franchise, or a gourmet selection, the burger is for you. I hope you will look to your local newspaper for their periodic listings and try some of the many burger places in your area. Maybe you, too, can join me and become a real Hamburcurion.

7

The World's Best Burgers

If you think it was hard to come up with a top ten list for the United States, just imagine what I had to go through to find the very best of the world's gourmet burgers! But with the input and assistance of some of the most notable chefs on earth, I can give you some idea of just how wonderful an international dining experience can be if you are a little adventurous. Whether you travel to familiar vacation places or to far-off and exotic lands, that seemingly familiar burger on the menu may be very different from what you expected.

So, to start you on your journey I have picked out my choices for the world's elite in burgers. And as a special bonus I am pleased to share the recipes for these marvelous taste delights. A special thanks to the great chefs who shared their secrets!

The Beijing Duck Burger

The Palace Hotel, Beijing, China

You have never had anything like it in your life, and I mean that as a compliment. I am very pleased and privileged to be able to include Master Chef Leslie Stronach's unique and exciting burger as one of the best in the world. The Palace does carry an exceptional all-beef hamburger on a sweet bun, but the Peking Duck Burger is absolutely fabulous. It shows what imagination can do when blended with talent. When in Beijing, consider stopping in at the Palace for a memorable meal. But if that's a little far to go for a meal, be sure to try Chef Stronach's recipe.

1 clove fresh garlic, chopped fine
1 green chili, chopped fine
¼ pound of leeks, finely chopped
1 pound duck meat, minced

Hamburger bun
Salt and pepper to taste
Duck skin (optional)

Sauté garlic, chili, and leek together until they are soft, and set aside to cool. In a bowl, mix the cooled garlic mixture with the ground duck meat. Form mixture into six individual patties. Grill over a charcoal or wood grill if possible; if not, broil under medium heat on oven rack. Toast the bun and serve. No condiments are needed, but you can use sweet-and-sour sauce, thickened soy sauce, or duck sauce for a real Oriental flavor. The duck skin can also be broiled until crisp and used as a garnish.

6 servings   *Courtesy of Leslie Stronach, Master Chef*

The Grand Gourmet Burger

Grand Veranda Restaurant, Stockholm, Sweden

If you thought that the Swedes ate ground beef only in Swedish meatballs you have probably never tried Executive Chef Manfred Mahnkopf's Grand Gourmet Burger. This is one juicy burger loaded with an all-natural flavor. The secret is Chef Mahnkopf's use of beef suet in his mixture. He also adds to the flavor by placing the patty on a warm sesame bun. This is the perfect meal for a cold winter night. So don't just admire the beautiful blondes in Sweden, visit the Grand Veranda in Stockholm and enjoy a beautiful meal also.

2 strips cured bacon
Salt
Fresh ground pepper
2 pounds fresh ground beef
½ pound beef suet
¼ cup coarsely chopped lettuce

6 slices sharp Cheddar cheese
(sliced)
Sesame seed buns
Thousand-Island dressing
Sweet pickle relish
Tomato slices

In an iron skillet cook the bacon over medium heat until crisp. Remove the bacon and set it aside. Salt and pepper the ground beef and mix with the beef suet. Form the mixture into six patties and place in the skillet with the bacon grease. Cook to desired doneness. Top with the Cheddar cheese and heat until melted. Toast the bun and coat the bottom with Thousand-Island dressing. Place patty on bun bottom and top with the bacon strips and chopped lettuce. Serve burgers garnished with the pickle relish and tomatoes.

6 servings   *Courtesy of Manfred Mahnkopf, master chef*

The Burger Cipriani

Cipriani Venezia, Venice, Italy

One of my favorite foods is spaghetti, and it wouldn't be spaghetti to my mind without a spicy Italian meatball. For a real treat, you must try this Italian burger creation. You will be completely impressed with the flavorful burger served in a very untraditional manner.

This burger has a unique flavor of its own, but when topped by Dr. Rusconi's spinach purée and Italian dressing, it will leave you with a memory to cherish. I am honored to include Master Chef Michael Lomonaco's recipe in my book.

1/2 pound lean ground beef
Worcestershire sauce
2 tablespoons virgin olive oil
2 tablespoons sweet butter
1 small rosemary sprig

1 teaspoon sifted flour
Salt and finely grated red pepper
1/4 teaspoon lemon juice
Sautéed spinach (optional)
Italian dressing (optional)

Mix the ground beef with a few drops of Worcestershire sauce. Form into a patty and set aside. In a skillet heat the oil, half of the butter, and the rosemary sprig. Coat the burger patty with the flour and place into the preheated skillet. Sauté the burger until golden brown on one side. Turn and continue to cook to desired degree of doneness. Sprinkle the salt and red pepper on top while cooking. Add lemon juice to burger top and the balance of the butter. Turn off the heat and cover for a couple of minutes. For a real Italian taste you can cover the burger with sautéed spinach and Italian dressing.

1 burger   *Courtesy Master Chef Michael Lomonaco*

Hamburger comme vous l'aimez

Café Wiltcher's, Brussels, Belgium

The name may be a mouthful, but so is the meal. The Wiltcher uses real Angus beef for its burger and flavors it with Madagascar green pepper.

In a city that hosts international groups such as NATO and is the home of the beautiful Grand Palais, you would expect to find the very best, and you do—at Mr. Gastone Di Domenico's restaurant. The restaurant is located in the beautiful Conrad Hilton Hotel and the ambience is as delightful as the food.

6 ounces fresh ground beef	1/4 cup canned tomatoes
Salt and pepper to taste	1/4 cup grated mozzarella cheese
1 small onion	Hamburger bun
1/4 teaspoon dried basil	1 slice cooked ham, boiled or baked

Season the ground beef with salt and pepper to taste and form into patty. Set patty aside. In a sauté pan cook the onion, basil, and tomatoes until done. Set the mixture aside keeping it warm. Grill or fry the burger patty to desired doneness. Top with mozzarella cheese and allow it to melt. Toast the bun. Place the cooked patty on the bottom half of the bun. Place the ham slice on top of the cheese and cover with the warm tomato-and-onion mixture. You are ready to serve.

1 burger   *Courtesy of Gastone Di Domenico*

The Frankfurt Hamburger

Arabella's, Frankfurt, Germany

Not to be outdone by their famous cousin, Hamburg, the birthplace of the hamburger, Frankfurt boasts one of the best burgers in the world. If Arabella's had been around when the burger was developed, we would be calling this favorite a frankfurt instead of a hamburg. (Now, isn't there some food that Frankfurt *is* famous for?)

You are sure to love the unique flavor of the spices and dressings in Director Holger Behrens's gourmet burger.

Hamburger bun	*1 teaspoon mayonnaise*
1 tablespoon sesame oil	*¼ teaspoon hot mustard*
2 leaves iceberg lettuce	*2 slices fresh tomato*
Salt and pepper	*4 slices peeled cucumber*
4 ounces fresh ground beef	*1 teaspoon sweet chili sauce*
½ cup vegetable oil	*½ teaspoon fresh grated*
4 thick slices onion	*horseradish*
1 beaten egg white	*2 strips cooked bacon*

Toast the bun. Heat the sesame oil in a skillet and sauté the lettuce. Salt and pepper to taste. Remove the lettuce from the frying pan and add the ground-beef patty to the heated pan. Cook the burger to desired doneness and set aside. Heat the vegetable oil to 425 degrees F. Dip onion rings in the egg white and deep-fry until brown. Cover the bottom of the bun with mayonnaise, hot mustard, and sautéed lettuce. Add the tomato and cucumber slices to the bun. Place the burger patty on top of these ingredients. Spread the top half of the bun with the sweet chili and sprinkle with horseradish. Top the burger with the bacon strips and the onion rings and place the bun on top. Serve. There is little need for additional condiments for this burger.

1 burger   *Courtesy Master Chef Holger Behrens*

The Melbourne Chargrilled Beef Burger

The Grand Hyatt, Melbourne, Australia

How could you have a book on food without including an Australian "bar-b" recipe? But here we came up with a winner. The Hyatt has an international reputation for excellence, and they take pride in serving an old-fashioned burger made from minced (not ground) beefsteak. They keep it simple by seasoning with only salt and pepper, and place their burger on a fresh bun. It is served with homemade potato chips. I promise you won't go away hungry. If you do, just tell Michelle Campbell—and I am sure she will fix you another one.

1/4 pound minced top round of beef *2 slices sweet onion*
Salt and pepper to taste *2 slices fresh tomato*
1 tablespoon butter *Hamburger bun*

Mix the ground beef with salt and pepper and form into patties. Melt the butter in a skillet over low heat, and sauté the onions until they are clear. Add the tomato slices to the skillet and cook until they are soft. Cook the burger patties on a charcoal or wood fire if possible for best taste. If not, broil on high in the oven close to the element. Cook to desired doneness. Baste the burgers with the butter and brown until crispy. Brush the bun with butter and toast over the flame or under the broiler. Place the patty on the bun and top with the tomato-and-onion mixture. Season to taste.

1 burger

*Courtesy Michelle Campbell
and the executive chef staff*

The Sydney Burger

The Park Hyatt, Sydney, Australia

A country as big as Australia is bound to have a variety of specialties when it comes to beef dishes. And the hamburger is just one of them. Citizens of Sydney boast the best burger in the outback, and after trying this one you might agree.

The secret toppings and seasonings used in Sydney are uniquely flavorful. So when doing a walk-about in the outback be sure to sample the local burgers, especially at the Park Hyatt.

¼ pound fresh-ground beef rump
2 tablespoons diced sweet onions
½ teaspoon salted butter
1 teaspoon whole-grain mustard

½ teaspoon Worcestershire sauce
¼ teaspoon paprika
Salt and pepper to taste
Hamburger bun

TOMATO CHUTNEY SAUCE

1 tablespoon virgin olive oil
½ teaspoon mustard seeds
¼ teaspoon cayenne pepper
¼ teaspoon turmeric
½ teaspoon cumin

1 teaspoon sugar
1 teaspoon white wine vinegar
1 fresh tomato, peeled and cut
 into 6 wedges

Prepare the tomato chutney: simmer the olive oil over low heat and add the mustard seeds, cayenne pepper, turmeric, and cumin. Cook for 15 minutes. Pour into a bowl and set aside.

Simmer the sugar and vinegar together until the sugar is melted. Place the tomato wedges in a metal bowl. Pour the oil and spices into the pan with the vinegar and sugar and heat the mixture. Pour over tomato and let stand for at least 3 hours before starting to cook the burgers.

When ready to start your burger patty preheat the grill or pan. Mix the ground beef with the onion, butter, mustard, Worcestershire sauce and paprika. Mix ingredients just before cooking as mustard and sauces will start to cure the meat. Blend mixture well and form into a patty. Cook to desired doneness, and season with salt and pepper. Toast the bun and place the cooked patty on the bottom half. Pour the hot tomato chutney over the burger, cover with top of bun, and serve.

1 burger   *Courtesy Sydney Hyatt executive staff*

◆ ◆ ◆ ◆ ◆

The Amerandari Gourmet Burger

Amerandari, Hong Kong, China

Hong Kong is one of my favorite cities in the world. Everything moves fast there, except dining. Then you take your time. And when you eat at Master Chef Andrew Skinner's restaurant, you want to savor every morsel.

Here the burger is made from imported Australian beef tenderloin trimmings and combined with a mixture of dried herbs. The flavor is enhanced with a dash of Tabasco and a little Lea & Perrins Worcestershire sauce. So enjoy the sights of bustling Hong Kong, but stop in at the Amerandari for a little taste of home.

3½ pounds beef tenderloin
  trimmings
2 teaspoons mixed dried herbs:
  parsley, sage, rosemary, thyme,
  oregano
Salt and pepper to taste
2 teaspoons Worcestershire sauce
Dash Tabasco sauce

1 small Spanish onion, sliced
Sesame-seed buns
2 tablespoons mayonnaise
2 tablespoons Dijon mustard
2 tablespoons chopped beetroot,
  poached
1 gherkin pickle, julienned

Combine the ground beef with the herbs, salt, pepper, Worcestershire sauce, and Tabasco sauce in a mixing bowl. Form into 6 patties and set aside. Heat frying pan over low heat and sauté the onion slices. Remove the cooked onions and fry the patty to desired doneness. Toast the bun. Spread the bottom of the bun with mayonnaise and Dijon mustard. Place the burger on top and top it off with beetroot, onions, and pickle; serve.

6 burgers   *Courtesy Executive Chef Andrew Skinner*

◆ ◆ ◆ ◆ ◆

The Israeli Hilton Burger

The Tel Aviv Deli at the Hilton, Tel Aviv, Israel

This kosher treat illustrates how, in Israel, they always do things a little differently. Here you will find a traditional American burger with a unique little twist. The onions are in the meat and not on it, and the burger includes the flavorful crunch of pine nuts, plus, for extra "zing," a little seltzer water. This is a really fun burger to make at home.

2 small sweet onions, chopped	*1 bunch fresh parsley*
1/4 cup pine nuts	*1 teaspoon cumin*
1 1/2 pounds chopped	*4 ounces seltzer water*
(not ground) beef shoulder	*6 hamburger buns*
6 ounces trimmed beef fat	*Salt and pepper to taste*

In an iron skillet sauté the onions until they are translucent. Add the pine nuts and cook for an additional minute. Set aside. In a mixing bowl combine the chopped beef, beef fat, sautéed onions, pine nuts, parsley, cumin, and seltzer. Blend well and form into 6 patties.

93

Grill or pan fry the burger to desired doneness and serve on bun with your choice of condiments and salt and pepper to taste. Brown mustard, pickled beets, and cole slaw are all good condiments to use.

6 burgers

Courtesy Andrew Jacobs
and his executive kitchen staff

◆　◆　◆　◆　◆

The Oberoi Burger

The Oberoi, Bombay, India

All the excitement and mystique of India are reflected in the Oberoi's burger. You will definitely have a hard time beating the flavor experience offered by this exotic burger. The combination of coriander, cumin, and green chili will definitely spice up your day. No need for traditional mustard here. And this burger is even better served on nan, a traditional Indian bread.

1 teaspoon vegetable oil
½ teaspoon finely chopped
  green chili
½ teaspoon coriander powder
½ teaspoon cumin powder

1 pound minced beef
2 teaspoons finely chopped
  sweet onions
½ teaspoon fresh coriander, chopped
Salt to taste

Heat the oil in a frying pan over medium heat. Add the chopped green chili and sauté until soft. Add the coriander powder and cumin powder to the chili and continue to sauté for 1 minute. Remove from heat and pour the mixture over the raw minced beef. Add the chopped onions and the fresh coriander to the beef mixture and blend well. Form into four patties. Place the patties on a preheated flat grill or in a preheated iron skillet and cook until well browned on the outside and to desired doneness. Add salt to taste. You can garnish with a curry sauce or an English chutney for a real Indian taste.

4 burgers

◆ ◆ ◆ ◆ ◆

Nan

3 ounces refined white flour
1 egg yolk
1 tablespoon and 2 teaspoons milk
½ teaspoon salt

1 teaspoon fresh coriander, chopped
1 teaspoon vegetable oil
½ teaspoon baking powder

Mix all the ingredients together in a large bowl. Divide the dough into 8 equal balls. Allow to stand at room temperature for 15 minutes. Roll out the dough balls to the same size as the meat patties. Heat a flat grill (or frying pan) over medium heat, and pan fry the dough patties until they are light brown. This bread is also great just by itself.

Makes 8 breads   *Courtesy Chef Zahid Hai*

The Barclay Burger

Le St. Honoré, Meridian, Rio de Janeiro, Brazil

The story goes that in the late 1970s a record impresario named Eddie Barclay decided to order his favorite food from one of the world's great chefs, Paul Bocuse. The chef delivered a burger that offered a flavor to satisfy the most jaded of palates. He used prime beef and topped it with black caviar. Now this is really something to try. The contrast between the salty caviar and the flavor of the prime beef is unique.

So if you attend Carneval, be sure to stop by the St. Honoré for a real treat.

6 ounces aged beef tenderloin
1 teaspoon lightly salted butter
¼ small sweet onion
Hamburger bun

1 tablespoon Dijon mustard
1 large leaf Belgian endive
1 tablespoon red or black caviar
½ teaspoon capers

Grind the tenderloin, and on the second pass through the grinder add the butter and mix it in well. (Since the tenderloin is nearly free of fat, the butter provides a tasty substitute.) Shape the meat into a patty. Dice the onion quarter into small squares. Brown the patty quickly on a hot skillet until crisp. Remove from the skillet and place on broiling pan. Finish cooking to desired doneness in the oven set at 375 degrees F. Lightly toast bun. Spread Dijon mustard on bottom of the bun and top with endive leaf. Remove burger from oven and allow to cool slightly; place patty on endive leaf, and spread caviar on top of burger. Sprinkle diced onions over the caviar. Sprinkle capers over the onions and top with bun. (This recipe doesn't call for salt since the salty flavor of the caviar eliminates the need for it.)

Makes 1 burger   *Courtesy Jaques Chevasson, Ritz Intercontinental*

The Royal Burger

The Vista Palace, Côte d'Azur, Monte Carlo

The Vista Palace is the most exciting place to eat in a city that boasts some of the world's most renowned restaurants. Here you'll find a burger fit for royalty, and I wouldn't be surprised if Princess Stephanie herself has enjoyed this treat. It has a fresh flavor and a killer aroma while it is cooking. They boast of pampering at the Vista Palace and they really mean it, so stop by when you visit the Côte d' Azur and live a little like a royal yourself.

1 small white onion
4 spring onions
1 tablespoon butter
¼ cup virgin olive oil
2 small seedless tomatoes or cored Beefsteak tomatoes, peeled and crushed

1 teaspoon sugar
1½ pounds lean ground beef rump
3 garlic cloves
4 hamburger buns
¼ pound mozzarella cheese
Sprig of parsley for garnish

Cut the onions into very thin slices, fry them in the butter until clear, and set them aside. Pour half of the olive oil into a frying pan and add the sugar and tomatoes. Cook until soft, then reduce heat and set aside. Mix the ground beef with the cooked onions and butter. Form into 4 patties. Set patties aside. Slice the garlic cloves into thin strips and fry until brown in the remaining olive oil.

Remove the garlic from the pan and place the burger patties in the garlic-flavored oil to cook. Cook burgers to desired doneness. Place patty on the bun and cover with cooked tomatoes. Top with mozzarella cheese, top the cheese with the fried garlic slices, and serve. This burger needs no additional condiments.

4 burgers   *Courtesy Patrice Glogg and the*
Vista Palace Hotel executive staff

8

Great American
Hamburger Recipes

There are thousands of ways to prepare hamburgers, each one unique. The flavors can range from very sweet to sour to hot and spicy. I have selected some of the most flavorful and unusual recipes from my collection for you to enjoy. First, however, a few notes on the cuts of beef used in burgers and safe ways of handling raw meat.

TIPS ON BUYING GROUND BEEF

All ground beef is not equal. When you go to the store you will find different grades of beef at different prices. The grade you select should be as lean as possible. The more seasonings you add, the less important the quality of the beef you select.

Regular Ground Beef or Chub Packs

Grocery stores and butcher shops offer a nongraded selection called fresh ground beef. It is made up from all different cuts and grades of beef. The grind includes pieces of round, chuck, loin, leg meat, neck meat, and scrapings from various bones of the carcass. This meat is generally relatively high in fat content and is a light pink color. When cooked it will shrink quite a lot because of the higher fat and moisture content.

Ground Chuck

Chuck is a flavorful cut of meat used primarily for stew meat and cube steak. The meat is darker pink in color than regular ground beef and has a lower fat content. The chuck cut is from the section of the beef between the neck and shoulder area.

Ground Round

This premium grade of beef is superior to ground chuck or regular ground beef. It comes from below the rump area of the beef and is used for steak and roasts. It is deeper red in color and richer in flavor than the chuck cuts. It is also generally more expensive, with less fat added to the grind.

Safe handling of ground meat

I can not emphasize enough that you must handle ground meat carefully. Health and safety measures must be followed. Here are the three basic rules to remember:

1. Keep meat refrigerated until you are ready to use it.
2. Wash all the surfaces that the meat touches, before and after you prepare it.
3. Make sure you cook the meat well enough (to an internal temperature of 140°F) to kill any Salmonella bacteria. Ground meat can be a rich breeding ground for germs.

The Farmer's Burger

MIDWEST

When a farmer and his family put in a full day's work in the fields they expect a filling meal. The Farmer's Burger is designed to be a main course for dinner. This is a hearty ground-beef meal with a fine gravy.

1 pound ground round or chuck
1 teaspoon dry mustard
1/2 teaspoon salt
1/4 teaspoon ground black pepper
2 tablespoons finely chopped green
*   bell pepper*

1/2 cup whole milk
1 tablespoon butter or margarine
1 can condensed cream of
*   mushroom soup*

In a medium bowl combine the ground beef, dry mustard, salt, pepper, green bell pepper, and milk. Mix together very well and form into four patties. In a medium frying pan melt the butter or margarine over medium heat. Add the burger patties and cook, turning occasionally, until they are browned on both sides. Pour the canned cream of mushroom soup over the burgers while cooking and simmer for 15 minutes. Serve with egg noodles, and spoon gravy over noodles.

4 servings

◆ ◆ ◆ ◆ ◆

American Pepper Steak

NEW ENGLAND

In Europe the finest restaurants serve filet mignon with black peppercorns. Here is an inexpensive way to prepare a ground beef dish with that European flavor at a fraction of the cost.

¼ cup boiling water

1 beef bouillon cube

2 pounds ground round or
  ground chuck

1 tablespoon Worcestershire sauce

2 teaspoons soy sauce

¼ teaspoon salt

½ teaspoon cracked black pepper

4 to 6 strips of bacon

In a medium mixing bowl pour boiling water over the bouillon cube and stir the mixture until it is fully dissolved. Add the ground beef, Worcestershire sauce, soy sauce, salt, and pepper. Mix the ingredients well until all the liquid is absorbed by the meat. Form meat into four to six patties, depending on how many people you are serving and the portion size you prefer. Wrap a strip of bacon around each patty and secure with a toothpick. Broil, grill, or pan-fry the patties until they are cooked to desired doneness.

4 to 6 servings

◆ ◆ ◆ ◆ ◆

Red Eye Cheeseburger

SOUTH

In the Deep South red eye gravy has long been used to spark up the flavor of meat. In this recipe the gravy, ham, and cheese are combined for a burger with great southern charm.

1½ pounds ground chuck or
  ground round

1 3 oz. piece of dry cured, country
  ham, cooked crisp and diced,
  fat reserved

½ cup grated Cheddar cheese

1 teaspoon of salt

¼ teaspoon ground black pepper

A few drops of coffee

In a medium mixing bowl combine the ground beef, diced ham, Cheddar cheese, salt, and black pepper. Mix lightly and form into four or six patties.

Heat a medium frying pan over medium heat and add the coffee and beef patties. Cook to desired doneness and serve on buns or on a plate.

4 to 6 servings

◆ ◆ ◆ ◆ ◆

Garden Beef Patty

WEST COAST

Here's an exciting new approach: a burger full of vegetables with a colorful appearance and a garden-fresh flavor.

1½ pounds ground chuck or
ground round
1 cup cooked potatoes, cut in
small cubes
1 small onion, chopped fine
¼ cup cooked carrots, julienned
¼ cup cooked green bell pepper,
chopped fine

1 teaspoon salt
¼ teaspoon ground black pepper
¼ cup evaporated milk
1 large egg
1 celery stalk, chopped fine
3 tablespoons butter or margarine

In a medium mixing bowl combine the ground beef, potatoes, onion, carrots, bell pepper, egg, evaporated milk, celery, salt, and black pepper. Mix together lightly and form into six thick, oblong patties. In a large frying pan melt the butter or margarine over medium heat. Add the patties and cook until done to your taste.

6 servings

Cheese Pocket Burgers

WEST COAST

The standard way to make a cheeseburger is to put all the cheese on top as a garnish. But cheese is even more flavorful *inside* the burger.

2 tablespoons whole milk
1/2 cup grated Cheddar cheese
1/2 cup soft bread crumbs
2 tablespoons chopped parsley
1 1/2 pounds ground chuck or
   ground round

1 small onion, chopped
2 teaspoons Worcestershire sauce
1 teaspoon salt
1/4 teaspoon ground black pepper
2 teaspoons butter or margarine

In a small mixing bowl combine the milk, Cheddar cheese, bread crumbs, and parsley. Mix together well, form into small balls, and set aside. In a medium mixing bowl combine the ground beef, onion, Worcestershire sauce, salt, and pepper, and mix well. Form meat mixture into four to six oblong patties with a shallow indentation in the middle of each.

Place a cheese ball in the center of each patty and fold both ends of the patty over until the ball is covered. Press the filled patty flat and reshape. In a medium frying pan melt the butter or margarine over medium heat and fry the patties until done to your taste. Serve on a bun or a plate.

4 to 6 servings

A-1 Burger

SOUTHWEST

Just as the advertisement says, A-1 Sauce goes great with steak. In this recipe we use it to add zip to the taste of a hamburger for a great sandwich that makes a hearty main course.

1½ pounds ground round or
   ground chuck
1 small onion, grated
1 teaspoon salt
¼ teaspoon ground black pepper

¼ teaspoon marjoram
¼ teaspoon parsley flakes
2 tablespoons butter or margarine
2 tablespoons A-1 Sauce

In a medium mixing bowl combine the ground beef, onion, salt, pepper, marjoram, and parsley. Mix together well and form into four to six patties, depending on the portion size you prefer. In a medium frying pan melt the butter or margarine. Place the formed beef patties in the frying pan and cook until done to your taste. Remove the cooked patties and set them aside. Add the A-1 Sauce to the drippings, mix together well, spoon the mixture over the burgers, and serve.

4 to 6 servings

◆ ◆ ◆ ◆ ◆

Georgia Pecan Burgers

SOUTH

Georgians love their home-grown pecans and use them to add flavor to almost everything. We have applied that approach to a Georgian burger favorite. This burger has a bit of crunch and an exciting new flavor.

1½ pounds ground round or
   ground chuck
1 teaspoon salt
¼ teaspoon ground black pepper

¼ teaspoon honey
½ cup chopped pecans
¼ teaspoon brown sugar
Honey mustard

In a medium mixing bowl combine the ground beef, salt, pepper, honey, pecans, and brown sugar. Mix well and form the mixture into four to six patties. Broil or pan fry the burgers to desired doneness. Serve on a bun with honey mustard for a new taste.

4 to 6 servings

◆ ◆ ◆ ◆ ◆

South Carolina Burger

SOUTHEAST

Carolinians love their homegrown pecans, too, but they're also known for their peaches, so it's not surprising that they enjoy a hamburger that combines both of these local flavors. This treat has a sweet taste that is great on a summer afternoon.

1½ pounds ground round or
   ground chuck
½ cup chopped pecans
1 small onion, chopped
1 teaspoon salt
⅛ teaspoon ground cloves

1 5-ounce baby food jar strained
   peaches
1 tablespoon brown sugar
2 teaspoons cider vinegar
⅛ teaspoon ground ginger

In a medium mixing bowl combine the ground beef, pecans, onion, salt, cloves, and 3 tablespoons of the strained peaches. Mix the ingredients together well and form into four to six patties, depending on preferred portion size. Broil or grill the patties until they are almost done to your taste. In a small mixing bowl combine the remaining peaches, brown sugar, vinegar, and ginger. This mixture will add a nice light glaze. Baste the burgers with it while they finish cooking.

4 to 6 servings.

◆　◆　◆　◆　◆

Old-Fashioned

MIDWEST

The one type of hamburger that hasn't changed over the centuries is the Old-Fashioned, a plump, juicy burger cooked over an open fire. Not everyone can take the time to fire up a wood-burning grill, though, so we developed a hamburger that gives you almost the same flavor and taste without all the mess and bother.

1½ pounds ground beef　　　　　*¼ teaspoon ground black pepper*
½ teaspoon liquid smoke　　　　　*1 teaspoon MSG*
½ teaspoon salt

In a medium mixing bowl combine the ground beef, liquid smoke, salt, pepper, and MSG. Mix together well and form into four big patties. Broil, fry, or grill until done to your taste. Serve on a bun with lettuce and tomato.

4 hearty servings

Peanut Butter Burger

WEST COAST

It's a very special treat that kids love. It combines two of their most favorite foods in the world—peanut butter and hamburgers. This delightful burger has all the flavor of hamburger combined with the chewiness of crunchy peanut butter.

1½ pounds ground chuck or
   ground round
1 small onion, grated
½ cup crunchy peanut butter

1 teaspoon MSG or Accent
½ teaspoon salt
Pinch of ground black pepper

In a medium mixing bowl combine the ground beef, grated onion, peanut butter, MSG, salt, and pepper. Form into six round patties. Fry until well browned on both sides and done to your taste. Serve on a bun with your choice of condiments.

6 servings

◆ ◆ ◆ ◆ ◆

Paul Revere Burger

NEW ENGLAND

In New England they take their hamburgers very seriously and like a distinctive flavor to their meats. When Paul Revere rode through the streets of Boston raising the alarm it might have been because he knew he had a special hamburger waiting for him at home. Try the Revere Burger and see if it's not worth riding hard for.

1/4 cup whole milk
1/2 cup soft bread crumbs
1 pound ground round or
   ground chuck

1/4 teaspoon brown mustard
1 teaspoon salt
1/4 teaspoon black pepper
1/4 teaspoon ground sage

In a medium mixing bowl combine the milk and bread crumbs; gently add the ground beef, mustard, salt, pepper, and sage. Mix lightly and form into four round patties. Broil the burgers until they are browned well on both sides and done to your taste. Serve on a fresh bun with your choice of condiments.

4 servings

◆ ◆ ◆ ◆ ◆

Indochine Burger

WEST COAST

The many young men who served in Southeast Asia grew to enjoy the taste of some of the traditional native cooking. We developed a hamburger that might help you enjoy the flavors of Vietnam in an ordinarily all-American dish.

1 1/2 pounds ground beef
1 1/2 tablespoons soy sauce
1/4 teaspoon ground ginger

1/2 teaspoon MSG
1 teaspoon grated lemon rind
1 tablespoon lemon juice

In a medium mixing bowl combine the ground beef, 1/2 tablespoon of the soy sauce, ginger, MSG, and lemon rind. Mix well and form into six round patties. Mix the balance of the soy sauce and lemon juice together in a small bowl and use it to baste the burgers as they cook. Grilling them will give them the most flavor but they can be broiled. Cook until done to your desired taste.

6 servings

Bangkok Burgers

WEST COAST

The exciting flavors of Thailand are captured in this blend of East and West. Our Bangkok Burger has a taste that is uniquely different from a more traditional sweet and sour flavor.

1½ pounds ground beef	¼ teaspoon ground black pepper
2 tablespoons brewed coffee	1 tablespoon butter or margarine
1 tablespoon salt	6 wooden skewers
Pinch of ginger	2 tablespoons soy sauce

In a medium mixing bowl combine the ground beef, brewed coffee, and salt. Mix well and form into four to six small rounded patties. Shape these around the wooden skewers. In a small frying pan melt the butter over medium heat and mix with ginger and pepper in the soy sauce. Brush the mixture on the patties and place in the broiler or on the grill. Cook until they are browned on all sides and done to your taste.

4 to 6 servings

◆　◆　◆　◆　◆

Beef Taco Burger

SOUTHWEST

Americans love the taste of Mexican food, but are not always adept at eating it on a tortilla. I have combined the flavor of Mexican food with the convenience of American food in this beef taco hamburger.

1 pound ground chuck or
   ground round
1 teaspoon chili powder
⅛ teaspoon ground black pepper

1 8-ounce can baked beans
¼ cup stuffed olives, chopped
1 cup grated Cheddar cheese
1 teaspoon salt

In a medium mixing bowl combine the ground beef, salt, chili powder, and black pepper. Mix well and form into four to six patties. In a separate small frying pan mash the baked beans slightly and combine with the olives, heating the mixture over a low heat. When hot, add the grated cheese and allow it to melt. Grill or broil the hamburger patties to desired doneness, place on a bun, and top each patty with the bean mixture. Garnish with chopped lettuce and serve with Mexican rice as a side dish.

4 to 6 servings

◆ ◆ ◆ ◆ ◆

Hawaiian Luau Burger

PACIFIC WEST

Even though Hawaii is one of the United States it is like an exotic foreign country when it comes to food. There they combine a dash of traditional island taste with the tradition of a mainland hamburger.

1 pound ground round or
   ground chuck
1 teaspoon salt
¼ teaspoon black pepper
1 fifteen-ounce can crushed
   pineapple

1 tablespoon yellow mustard
1 teaspoon brown sugar
¼ teaspoon ground ginger
2 tablespoons dried coconut flakes
   for garnish

In a medium mixing bowl combine the ground beef, salt, and pepper. Form into four round patties and set aside. In a small mixing bowl combine the crushed pineapple, mustard, brown sugar, and ginger and mix well. Fry the hamburgers over medium heat in a large frying pan. Cover the patties with most of the pineapple mixture and turn frequently.

When the meat is almost done pour any remaining pineapple mixture over the patties and cook for an additional 4 minutes. Sprinkle with coconut flakes when finished.

Serve on a plate, spooning the cooked pineapple mixture over the top of the burgers. This tastes great over white rice.

4 servings

◆ ◆ ◆ ◆ ◆

Creole Burger

SOUTH

Blackened with spices that bring your taste buds alive, this burger makes you feel that you are sitting on Bourbon Street in New Orleans and listening to Dixieland jazz.

1½ pounds of ground round or ground chuck
½ teaspoon salt
¼ teaspoon MSG or Accent
1½ tablespoons Cajun seasoning

¼ teaspoon Tabasco sauce (optional; for those who like a very hot taste)
2 tablespoons butter or margarine

In a medium mixing bowl combine the ground beef, salt, MSG, and ½ teaspoon of the Cajun seasoning. Add Tabasco sauce if desired. Blend the mixture well and form into six patties. In a medium frying pan melt the butter over a high heat. Sprinkle both sides of the patties with the balance of the Cajun seasonings. Place the patties in the frying pan and cook until done to your taste. Serve on a bun with lettuce and tomato.

6 servings

◆ ◆ ◆ ◆ ◆

French Brie Burger

NORTHEAST

Country French flavor blended with the all-American burger makes for a new type of taste that will remind you of a dish served in a Parisian café.

1½ pounds ground beef	*¼ teaspoon chopped parsley*
Pinch of marjoram	*2 tablespoons butter or margarine*
¼ teaspoon salt	*6 ounces Brie*
¼ teaspoon ground black pepper	

In a medium mixing bowl combine the ground beef, marjoram, salt, pepper, and parsley. Form the mixture into six patties. Heat a medium frying pan over medium heat and melt the butter or margarine. Cook the patties in the frying pan until they are browned on both sides. Top them with the Brie while they are still in the frying pan. Serve hot with the cheese melted, on French bread for a true French taste.

6 servings

Burger Italiano

NORTHEAST

The spices that make Italian meatballs so popular are added to our hamburger patty for a traditional Italian flavor and an exciting meal.

1½ pounds ground round or
   ground chuck
¼ teaspoon salt
⅛ teaspoon dried oregano
¼ teaspoon coarse-ground
   black pepper
⅛ teaspoon dried rosemary

¼ teaspoon garlic powder
⅛ teaspoon thyme
¼ cup Italian seasoned breadcrumbs
3 tablespoons olive oil
¼ cup grated Parmesan-and-romano
   cheese mix

In a medium mixing bowl combine the ground beef, salt, oregano, black pepper, rosemary, garlic powder, and thyme. Mix the ingredients together well and form into six patties. Press the bread crumbs onto the patties until they are coated. In a medium frying pan heat the oil over low to medium heat and sauté the burgers until done to your taste. Top the hot Italiano burgers with the grated Parmesan and romano cheese and serve.

6 servings

Burger Pepperoni

MIDWEST

Combine the flavors of two of the most popular foods for a special pizzaburger combination sure to please everyone at your table.

1½ pounds ground round or
  ground chuck
¼ teaspoon salt
¼ teaspoon ground black pepper
¼ teaspoon garlic

¼ teaspoon oregano
½ cup prepared pizza sauce
¼ cup grated mozzarella cheese
4 ounces sliced pepperoni

In a medium mixing bowl combine the ground beef, salt, pepper, garlic, and oregano. Mix the ingredients well and form into six patties. Place the patties on a broiler and cook on both sides until almost done. Spoon the pizza sauce over the top of the cooked burgers and top with the grated mozzarella. Place the pepperoni slices on top of the cheese and broil until the cheese is melted and starting to brown. Serve on a bun or Italian bread.

6 servings

Burger Stroganoff

NORTHEAST

Beef Stroganoff is one of the world's most popular dishes. We thought that you might enjoy the taste of our American version, a hamburger blended with mushrooms, onion, and sour cream.

1½ pounds ground round or
   ground chuck
¼ teaspoon salt
¼ teaspoon ground black pepper
¼ teaspoon MSG or Accent
1 teaspoon parsley flakes

¼ teaspoon garlic powder
2 tablespoons cooking sherry
2 tablespoons vegetable oil
1 small onion, sliced
5-ounce can mushroom pieces
½ cup sour cream

In a medium mixing bowl combine the ground beef, salt, pepper, MSG, parsley, garlic powder, and 1 tablespoon of the cooking sherry. Mix the ingredients well, form into six patties, and set them aside. In a small frying pan heat the oil over a medium heat. Sauté the onions until they are soft. Add the remaining tablespoon of cooking sherry and the drained mushrooms to the onions. Sauté over low heat until the mixture is heated through. Place the patties under the broiler and cook until they are browned on both sides.

When done to taste, remove the burgers from the broiling pan. Add the sour cream to the broiling pan drippings and blend it with the onion-mushroom mixture. Spoon some over the burgers and serve. Serve with noodles topped with remaining onion-mushroom mixture.

6 servings

Barbecue Burger

SOUTHWEST

Barbecue and hamburgers go together like fresh air and sunshine. We have taken the best of outdoor cooking and put it together in one great recipe for your dining pleasure. This is a great burger to fix on those rainy days when you long for the outdoors.

*1½ pounds ground round or
  ground chuck*
¼ teaspoon salt
¼ teaspoon ground black pepper
*2 tablespoons liquid smoke
  (hickory or mesquite)*

½ cup your favorite barbecue sauce
3 tablespoons vegetable oil
1 small onion, chopped
Hamburger buns
Onion slices

In a medium mixing bowl combine the ground beef, salt, pepper, liquid smoke, and 1 tablespoon of the barbecue sauce. Mix well and set aside. In a medium frying pan heat the oil and sauté the chopped onion. When browned well remove from the frying pan and combine with the ground beef. Mix together well and form into four to six patties. Place the patties on a grill or broiler. Baste with remaining barbecue sauce while cooking. Serve on a bun with a slice of raw onion.

4 to 6 servings

Alpine Burger

NORTHWEST

Here's a little taste of the Alps in the shape of a hamburger. Nothing is better than this hearty meal to top off a day of skiing or hiking.

1 1/2 pounds ground beef	2 teaspoons dried parsley
1/4 teaspoon salt	1 6-ounce can sauerkraut
1/4 teaspoon ground black pepper	6 slices Swiss cheese

In a medium mixing bowl combine the ground beef, salt, pepper and parsley. Mix well and form into six patties. Place the burgers in a medium frying pan and cook to desired doneness on both sides. Add the sauerkraut to the frying pan and heat in the hamburger juices. Place the Swiss cheese slices on top of the burgers and heat until they begin to melt. Top the cheese with the heated sauerkraut and serve.

6 servings

9

Hamburgers and Ground Beef Recipes From Around the World

◆ ◆ ◆ ◆ ◆

Pampas Beef Loaf

ARGENTINA

From the great Pampas of Argentina we bring the meal that gauchos enjoy during their cattle drives. Like the cowboys of the American west, the cattlemen in this South American country butcher their own beef while on the trail and sometimes hunt wild pigs on the plains. They have developed meals with hearty flavor and a bold taste.

1 large egg, beaten	3 tablespoons sliced green olives
½ cup whole milk	2 tablespoons chopped onion
1 cup dry bread crumbs	2 teaspoons salt
1½ pounds ground beef	¼ teaspoon ground black pepper
¼ pound ground pork	¼ cup chili sauce

In a medium mixing bowl combine the beaten egg and the milk. Mix together well and add the bread crumbs. Allow crumbs to soak for 10 minutes. Add the ground beef, ground pork, olives, onion, salt, and pepper. Blend together and form into six thick patties or one oblong loaf. Place the meat loaf or patties in a greased shallow baking dish and cover with the chili sauce. Place in the oven at 350 degrees F. for 30 minutes for patties, 1 hour for loaf.

6 to 8 servings

◆ ◆ ◆ ◆ ◆

Esprit Meat Loaf

AUSTRIA

High in the Alps, Austria is a country with some of the world's most beautiful lakes and a history of producing wonderful composers. They also have a hamburger that is guaranteed to please your palate after a day of skiing or ice skating.

1 pound ground round or ground chuck	1/4 teaspoon ground black pepper
1 large egg	1 teaspoon Worcestershire sauce
1/4 cup whole milk	1 small head cauliflower
1/2 cup dry bread crumbs	1 cup grated sharp Cheddar cheese
1/2 cup chopped onions	1 cup evaporated milk
1/2 teaspoon salt	3 tomatoes, sliced

Preheat over to 350 degrees F. In a medium mixing bowl combine the ground beef, egg, milk, bread crumbs, onions, salt, pepper, and Worcestershire sauce. Mold the mixture into a ring in a round baking dish, leaving space in the center.

Parboil the cauliflower head for 5 minutes and place it in the center of the meat loaf ring. Mix the cheese and milk in a separate mixing bowl and pour the mixture over the cauliflower. Bake for 45 minutes. Arrange the tomato slices on top of the meat loaf and continue baking for an additional 5 minutes. Serve with buttered parsley noodles or spaetzle.

4 servings

◆ ◆ ◆ ◆ ◆

Beef-Stuffed Zucchini
(Ahmaithar Thut)

BURMA

Burma, in Southeast Asia, is noted for its tropical splendor and food that is a blend of creative flavor and design.

1 pound ground round or
*   ground chuck*
1 medium onion, chopped
1 teaspoon salt
1 tablespoon paprika
1 tablespoon flour

½ teaspoon ground black pepper
4 large zucchini (6 inches long, 4
*   inches in circumference)*
¼ cup vegetable oil
½ cup water

In a medium mixing bowl combine the ground beef, onion, salt, paprika, flour, and pepper. Mix together well and set aside. Wash the zucchini and cut them cross-wise into 2-inch-thick rounds. Scrape out the seeds in the center, leaving a wall that is about ¼ inch thick all the way around. Stuff the meat mixture into the center of the squash pieces. In a medium frying pan heat the oil over medium heat. Add the water to the pan and place the zucchini pieces in the mixture. Simmer them gently until the water evaporates and the oil remains, turning frequently to allow for cooking on both sides. Stir-fry the pieces gently until they are soft in the middle, then serve.

5 to 6 servings

◆ ◆ ◆ ◆ ◆

Baked Stuffed Hamburger

CANADA

Our neighbor to the north is a vast country that stretches from ocean to ocean. In this cool clime, foods have to be hearty and filling to satisfy Canadian tastes.

1½ *pounds ground chuck or*	4 *tablespoons chopped parsley*
ground round	1½ *teaspoons salt*
4 *tablespoons chopped onion*	¼ *cup vegetable oil*

STUFFING

1½ *cups soft bread crumbs*	½ *teaspoon salt*
½ *cup chopped peanuts*	¼ *teaspoon black pepper*
¼ *cup chopped walnuts*	2 *tablespoons water*

TOPPING

6 *slices Canadian bacon*	3 *tomato slices*

Preheat oven to 350 degrees F. In a medium mixing bowl combine the ground beef, onions, parsley, salt, and vegetable oil. Mix together lightly and set aside. To make the stuffing, combine in a separate mixing bowl the bread crumbs, peanuts,

walnuts, salt, pepper, and water, and mix well. In a 2-quart baking dish place a
layer of stuffing mixture, then a layer of ground-beef mixture, and a final layer of
stuffing mixture. Top with the bacon slices and arrange the tomato slices on top of
the bacon. Cover, and bake for 1 hour. Uncover and bake for an additional 30
minutes. Serve with mashed potatoes and a vegetable.

6 servings

◆ ◆ ◆ ◆ ◆

Meatballs Oriental

CHINA

Home of one of the world's oldest civilizations, China has always been a leader in
good cooking. Chinese cuisine employs ground beef and pork in many traditional
recipes.

1½ pounds ground beef *¼ cup sliced water chestnuts*
2 large eggs *1 10¼-ounce can beef broth*
1½ teaspoons salt *1 teaspoon sugar*
¼ teaspoon black pepper *1 pound bean sprouts*
3 tablespoons vegetable oil *2 tablespoons cornstarch*
1 celery stalk, sliced cross-wise *1 tablespoon water*
2 large onions, sliced *3 tablespoons soy sauce*

In a mixing bowl combine the ground beef, eggs, salt, and pepper. Mix well and
form into egg-size meatballs. In a medium frying pan heat the oil over medium
heat. Brown the meatballs, remove them from the pan, and set aside to drain on
paper towels. Add the celery, onions, and water chestnuts to the drippings and
cook over a medium heat. Cook until the onions are soft, then add the beef broth,

sugar, bean sprouts, and meatballs.

Cover and simmer for 15 minutes. Stir frequently. In a small mixing bowl combine the cornstarch, water, and soy sauce. Mix well and pour into the pan. Heat until the broth has thickened, and serve with white rice.

6 servings

◆ ◆ ◆ ◆ ◆

Blue Cheese and Veal

CORSICA

This small island off the coast of France has a very big political influence on the rest of the world. The delights of Corsican food are internationally known.

2 pounds ground veal
$1/3$ teaspoon ground white pepper
1 teaspoon salt
$1/2$ cup sour cream
$1/4$ cup crumbled blue cheese

In a medium mixing bowl combine the ground veal, pepper, and salt. Mix lightly and form into six patties. Place the veal patties on a broiler close to the flame or heating element and cook quickly until both sides are brown. Remove from broiler. While the patties are cooking mix the sour cream and blue cheese together in a small bowl. Spoon $1^1/2$ tablespoons of the cheese mixture on top of the burgers and place back under the broiler for 2 minutes. Serve with baked potato and a green vegetable.

6 servings

Beef With Olives and Almonds
(Picadillo)

CUBA

Cubs is one of the most beautiful islands in the world, with a tropical climate, a strong Spanish influence, and flavorful meals. With slight variations, this delightful recipe is native to almost every Latin country in the world.

1 pound ground chuck or
   ground round
1 medium onion, chopped
1 garlic clove, chopped
1 small green bell pepper, chopped
1/4 cup raisins
1 1/2 teaspoons salt

Pinch of cinnamon
Pinch of ground cloves
1/4 cup chopped green olives
1/4 cup chopped pimientos
2 large tomatoes, chopped
1/4 cup slivered almonds

In a large frying pan cook ground beef, onion, and garlic over medium heat until the meat is browned. Drain off the excess fat and add the bell pepper, raisins, salt, cinnamon, cloves, olives, pimiento, and tomatoes. Mix together well and simmer for 10 minutes. Raise the heat and add the almonds. Cook for 3 minutes or until almonds are golden. Serve immediately with white or saffron rice.

6 servings

Danish Meat Patties

DENMARK

The Danes have been exporting their recipes ever since the Vikings began their expeditions across the world. They have always enjoyed their beef, and this Danish hamburger is a unique reflection of their robust life style.

1 pound ground round or
   ground chuck
1 medium onion, chopped
2 tablespoons flour
¹/₄ cup club soda
1 large egg, beaten
¹/₄ teaspoon ground black pepper
1 teaspoon salt

2 tablespoons vegetable oil
2 pounds small potatoes,
   peeled and boiled
2 tablespoons butter or margarine,
   melted
¹/₄ cup sour cream
3 tablespoons chopped chives

In a large mixing bowl combine the ground beef and onion. Add the flour, club soda, egg, black pepper, and salt. Mix together well and chill for an hour. Shape into four oval patties; dust lightly with additional flour. In a large frying pan heat the oil over medium heat, cook the patties until browned on both sides. Remove the patties from the frying pan and drain on paper towels.

Place the boiled potatoes in the frying pan and cook for an additional 20 minutes over low heat. Replace the burgers and cook until heated through. Pour the melted butter or margarine over the potatoes and top with chives and sour cream. Serve with a vegetable.

4 servings

Beef and Kidney Pie

ENGLAND

One of the best-known dishes of England is the meat pie. This dish dates back to a time when the prime cuts of meat were reserved for royalty and the common folk were left with the scrapings or tougher pieces for their meals. These small cubes provided the same nutritional benefits as the choicer cuts, but required more elaborate preparation to make them palatable.

This recipe is not especially complicated, requires no special expertise in the kitchen, and is very forgiving if it has to sit for a while before it is served.

2 medium onions, chopped into fine cubes
2 tablespoons cooking oil
2 pounds coarse-ground round or coarse-ground chuck
1/2 pound beef or veal kidneys
1 teaspoon flour
3 tablespoons Worcestershire sauce

Salt to taste
Coarse-ground black pepper to taste
1 bay leaf
1 1/2 teaspoons rosemary
1/2 teaspoon thyme
1 6-ounce bottle stout (optional)
2 cups mushrooms, chopped into small pieces

Preheat the oven to 350 degrees F. In a frying pan, sauté the onions in the oil until they are soft; then place them in a 2-quart casserole dish. Dust the ground beef and the kidneys with the flour and brown in the frying pan. Add a little more oil if necessary. Add the meat to the casserole dish and mix with the onions. Spoon the Worcestershire sauce on top and sprinkle with salt and pepper. Crush the bay leaf and mix with the rosemary and thyme; sprinkle over the meat mixture. For a more traditional taste you may add stout to the mixture.

Cover the casserole and bake for 2 hours. Uncover and continue to bake for an additional hour. Add chopped mushrooms and cook for 30 minutes more. Add a little water to thin the sauce if it becomes too thick. Serve with a vegetable and boiled new potatoes.

6 servings

◆ ◆ ◆ ◆ ◆

Cabbage Rolls

FINLAND

Finland is located to the far north, and its people have learned to survive severe cold and extreme conditions. To help them get through cold weather they have developed warming, tasty, and filling meals, featuring main courses like this one.

12 large cabbage leaves
1 pound ground beef
1 cup cooked rice
1 medium onion, chopped fine
1/4 teaspoon ground black pepper
1 large egg
1/2 cup whole milk
1 teaspoon chopped parsley

1 teaspoon salt
2 tablespoons butter or margarine
2 tablespoons brown sugar
1 bay leaf
1 can condensed tomato soup
4 whole cloves
1/2 soup can water

Wash the cabbage leaves well and place in a saucepan of boiling, salted water for 5 minutes or until they are soft. Drain and trim away the thick center vein. Set aside to cool. In a medium mixing bowl add the ground beef, cooked rice, half of the onion, black pepper, egg, milk, parsley and salt. Mix thoroughly. Pinch off an egg-size amount of meat and place it in the center of a cabbage leaf. Wrap the leaf around the meat mixture and fasten with a toothpick.

In a medium frying pan melt the butter or margarine. Place the cabbage leaves in the melted butter and brown evenly on all sides. Add the brown sugar, tomato soup, remaining onion, bay leaf, cloves, and water. Cover and simmer for 1 hour or a little longer, until meat is brown. Serve with white rice and a salad.

6 servings

◆　◆　◆　◆　◆

French Pastry Loaf

FRANCE

The world has always hailed France as a leader in culinary arts. French meals are explosive with flavor and color. When it comes to the ancient hamburger they are no different. This French version is sure to draw raves from your family.

PASTRY

2 cups flour
1 teaspoon salt

6 tablespoons cold water
²/₃ cup chilled shortening

MEAT MIXTURE

1 pound ground veal
3 tablespoons chopped pimiento
1¹/₂ teaspoons salt
¹/₈ teaspoon black pepper
3 tablespoons chopped green olives
1 tablespoon cooking sherry

6 tablespoons butter
6 tablespoons flour
1 cup beef stock
1 egg, lightly beaten and diluted with a little water
¹/₄ cup sautéed mushrooms

For the pastry: In a medium mixing bowl mix together the flour and salt. In a separate mixing bowl place ⅓ cup of the flour mixture and blend with ¼ cup of the cold water. Blend to form a paste. In the first mixing bowl add the shortening to the remaining flour-and-salt mixture and blend well.

Combine the contents of the two mixing bowls and blend them together into a dough. Chill in the refrigerator while preparing the meat mixture.

For the meat mixture: In a medium mixing bowl combine the ground veal, pimiento, salt, pepper, olives and sherry. Set aside. In a large frying pan melt the butter over low heat. Add the flour gradually and mix until smooth. Add the beef stock and continue cooking and stirring until very thick. Add a little of the stock mixture to the meat, mix well, and shape into an oblong loaf. Refrigerate the loaf for 3 hours.

Preheat oven to 425 degrees F. Roll the chilled pastry dough into an oblong shape and place the chilled meat roll in the center. Fold the pastry over the meat and seal the ends.

Brush the pastry with beaten egg, bake for about an hour or until nicely browned, and top with the sautéed mushrooms. Serve with a salad and vegetable.

6 servings

◆   ◆   ◆   ◆   ◆

Rheinpfaltz Poached Meatballs

GERMANY

The land of the Goths and the Huns has always been a place of mystery and innovation. The Germans gave us the hamburger as we know it today as well as the hot dog, sausages, and many other foods that are now standards in the culinary world.

1 pound ground chuck or
   ground round
1/2 pound ground pork
1 large egg
1 3/4 cups soft, fine bread crumbs
   (Kaiser roll, French or Italian
   bread) soaked in 1/3 cup of
   water for 5 minutes.

2 tablespoons chopped parsley
1/2 teaspoon marjoram
1/4 teaspoon ground cloves
1/4 teaspoon ground nutmeg
1 teaspoon salt
1/4 teaspoon ground black pepper
7 cups beef broth

In a medium mixing bowl combine the ground beef, ground pork, egg, bread crumbs, parsley, marjoram, cloves, nutmeg, salt, and pepper. Mix together thoroughly and refrigerate for at least an hour.

Pour the beef broth into a medium saucepan and heat to a simmer over low heat. Form the meat mixture into meatballs about the size of large eggs and roll tightly.

As the broth starts to steam gently ease the meatballs into the broth. Distribute them so that they do not touch, and simmer uncovered for 10 minutes.

Cover and simmer for an additional 10 minutes or until the meatballs start to float in the broth. Remove them from the broth and serve. If you need to keep the first batch warm while you cook a second batch, be sure to keep them tightly wrapped in foil so they don't dry out.

Serve with spaetzle noodles and spoon the broth over the noodles for a traditional meal.

6 servings

Stuffed Grape Leaves

GREECE

It is not surprising that a civilization that has brought the world so much in art, sculpture, philosophy, and culture has also been inventive in the culinary arts.

1 pound ground lamb or ground beef	2 tablespoons olive oil
1/2 cup chopped scallions	1/4 cup chopped almonds
1/4 cup currants	1 1-pound jar grape leaves
2 cups cooked white rice	1/4 cup lemon juice
1/2 teaspoon salt	1 10-ounce can beef broth
2 tablespoons chopped parsley	1 cup water
	3 lemons, cut in wedges

In a medium frying pan place the ground lamb or beef, the scallions, and the currants, and cook over medium heat until browned. Remove the meat, drain off excess fat.

In a large mixing bowl combine the meat, rice, salt, parsley, olive oil, and almonds, and mix well. Refrigerate for 30 minutes.

Meanwhile drain off the liquid from the canned grape leaves, rinse the leaves in cold water, and set them on a paper towel to dry. When they are dry lay them flat with the shiny side down and trim off any stems.

Place 1 teaspoonful of the meat mixture toward the bottom of one leaf and fold the bottom over the mixture. Then carefully fold the sides of the leaf toward the middle and roll the leaf forward. Proceed until all leaves are filled. Lay the folded grape leaves side by side and seam-side down in a large saucepan. It is okay to add a second or third layer of filled leaves to the pan. Sprinkle each layer with lemon juice.

Pour the beef broth and water over the rolls. Place a plate or round dish on top of the rolls to keep them from separating while cooking. Cover the saucepan and cook for about an hour over low heat. Remove from saucepan and drain off all the liquid. Serve hot or cold, topped with the lemon wedges as an appetizer or as an entrée.

6 servings as an entrée; 12 appetizer servings

◆ ◆ ◆ ◆ ◆

Tamale Pie

GUATEMALA

This small Central American country has a rich Spanish history threaded through its culture. Many Guatemalan dishes have evolved from Spanish ones, modified to suit an almost tropical climate.

3 tablespoons vegetable oil
¼ cup chopped green bell pepper
¼ cup chopped onion
1 pound ground round or ground chuck
1 teaspoon salt
¼ teaspoon black pepper
1 bay leaf

2 tablespoons chopped jalapeño pepper (optional, for hot flavor only)
1 15½-ounce can of stewed tomatoes
1 14½-ounce can whole kernel corn
½ cup cornmeal

In a large frying pan heat the oil over low heat. Add the bell pepper and onion and cook until they are soft but not yet brown. Add the ground beef and continue to cook until the meat is browned, mixing it evenly with the onion, salt, pepper, bay leaf, and jalapeños. Add the tomatoes, corn, and cornmeal; mix together well. Pour the mixture into a greased baking dish and bake at 350 degrees F. for 1 hour. Serve with Spanish rice and corn tortillas.

6 servings

◆ ◆ ◆ ◆ ◆

Stuffed Bell Peppers

HUNGARY

From the grand balls that were once held in the courts of Buda and Pest come some of the most flavorful and attractive meals around today.

1 pound ground beef
¼ teaspoon salt
¼ teaspoon Hungarian paprika
¼ teaspoon chopped parsley
4 large green bell peppers
1 15½-ounce can stewed tomatoes
1 bay leaf

In a medium frying pan combine the ground beef, salt, paprika, and parsley. Cook over a low heat until the ground beef starts to lose its red color. Remove from heat and set aside. Wash and core the green bell peppers, removing the seeds and interior sections but leaving the outer shell complete. Spoon the slightly cooked meat mixture into the bell peppers. Place them into a shallow baking dish. Preheat the oven to 325 degrees F. Pour the stewed tomatoes, bay leaf, and juice from the can over peppers. Bake in the oven for 45 minutes, basting the peppers with the juices from the baking dish as the meat cooks.

6 servings

Keema Curry

INDIA

The mysterious land of India has always been a source of exotic mystery, with food like none other in the world. Indian spices and flavorings will excite your palate and make your meal memorable.

4 tablespoons butter or margarine
2 medium onions, chopped
1 large garlic clove, mashed
1½ tablespoons curry powder
1 pound ground lamb or
   ground beef
½ teaspoon ground ginger

¼ teaspoon ground cloves
1½ cups peeled canned tomatoes
⅓ cup of the juice from the canned
   tomatoes
1½ teaspoons salt
1 bay leaf
¾ cup frozen peas

Heat butter or margarine in a medium frying pan over medium heat. Add onions, garlic, curry powder. Cover and cook over low heat for 10 to 15 minutes or until the onions are tender.

Raise heat to medium and crumble the ground lamb or beef over the mixture. Sprinkle in the ginger and cloves and stir until the meat loses its red color. Add the tomatoes, tomato liquid, salt, bay leaf, and peas. Cover and simmer until the peas are tender, about 15 to 20 minutes.

For a traditional meal, serve with rice and with raw vegetables dipped in a yogurt sauce.

6 servings

Apple-Burger Meatballs

ISRAEL

In a land that has spawned so many epic changes we find recipes that are as unique as its people are diverse. In Israel the hamburger is prepared many, many ways—all of them interesting and different.

2 medium apples
   (Macintosh are best)
1½ pounds ground beef
1 teaspoon onion salt
Pinch of white pepper
¼ teaspoon ground cloves
1 small egg
½ cup fine dry bread crumbs

2 tablespoons flour
1 cup hot water
2 chicken bouillon cubes
2 tablespoons raisins
¼ teaspoon lemon juice
1 tablespoon cold water
1½ teaspoons cornstarch

Peel, core, quarter the apples, and chop into small pieces. Place the chopped apples in a large mixing bowl and add the ground beef, onion salt, white pepper, cloves, egg, and bread crumbs. Mix the ingredients together well and shape into small balls. Roll the balls in the flour to coat them. Set the meatballs aside.

Heat the butter or margarine in a medium frying pan over medium heat. Add the almonds and heat them until they are brown. Remove the almonds and set them aside. Add the meatballs to the heated oil and brown. Remove them from the pan and allow them to cool. Add the hot water to the pan, the bouillon cubes, raisins, lemon juice, and cooled almonds. Mix together well and add meatballs. In a separate bowl blend cold water and cornstarch until smooth. Add to the meatball mixture in the frying pan and mix in. Cook for a minute or so longer until the sauce thickens.

For a complete meal serve with brown rice and zucchini squash.

6 servings

Parmesan Burger

ITALY

Since before Rome conquered most of the world, Italy has been developing gastronomic creations that spread across the conquered lands. Italians quickly grasped the benefits of using ground beef in their meals.

1½ pounds ground round
½ teaspoon salt
¼ teaspoon ground black pepper
¼ cup flour
2 large eggs, beaten
1 cup dry Italian bread crumbs

1 tablespoon olive oil
½ cup grated mozzarella cheese
1 4-ounce can mushroom pieces
1 28-ounce jar tomato sauce
3 tablespoons grated Parmesan cheese

In a medium mixing bowl combine the ground beef, salt, and pepper. Mix lightly and shape into 6 patties. Dust each patty with flour and dip them into the beaten eggs. Gently press the bread crumbs into the patties. Heat the olive oil over a low heat in a medium frying pan. Place the patties in the pan and cook until browned on both sides. Remove from the frying pan and place in a baking dish. Sprinkle the top of the patties with mozzarella. Place the mushroom pieces on top of the cheese and cover with the tomato sauce. Sprinkle with Parmesan cheese on top. Bake in the oven for 25 minutes at 325 degrees F. or until the cheese is melted. Serve with spaghetti.

6 servings

Tofu Burgers

JAPAN

The Japanese have always honored the simplicity of all things in their life. Even their hamburger makes a simple yet tasty meal.

1 block of soft tofu
1 pound ground round or
    ground chuck
1 scallion, chopped
¼ teaspoon ginger

3 tablespoons flour
¼ teaspoon salt
1 egg, blended, not beaten
1 tablespoon vegetable oil
1½ tablespoons soy sauce

Cut the tofu block into 3 half-inch strips and, using a paper towel, press out the moisture. Set aside and let the tofu stand. In a medium mixing bowl combine the ground beef, scallion, ginger, tofu, flour, salt and egg, and mix well. Form into six patties. In a large frying pan heat the oil over medium heat. Sauté the tofu burgers in the frying pan, and coat with the soy sauce until they are browned and cooked to desired doneness.

Serve on a bun with hot Oriental mustard.

6 servings

137

Burrito

MEXICO

Mexican food has become one of the most popular ethnic foods in the world. The Mexicans have some very inventive ways to use ground meats of all kinds. This ever-popular menu item is the Mexican equivalent of a cheeseburger.

1½ pounds ground beef
1 large onion, chopped
¼ cup diced green bell pepper
1 tablespoon chili powder
1½ tablespoons flour
1 8-ounce can peeled tomatoes
1½ cups water

1½ teaspoons salt
1½ teaspoons sugar
1 teaspoon cumin
1 12-ounce package of burrito size flour tortillas
½ cup grated Cheddar cheese

In a large frying pan brown the ground beef. Add the onion, bell pepper, and chili powder, and cook until the onion is soft. Sprinkle the flour over the top and mix in well. Add the tomatoes, water, salt, sugar, and cumin. Bring to a boil, then reduce the heat and allow to simmer for 15 minutes or until thickened. Allow to stand while heating the tortillas.

In a small frying pan heat the tortillas on both sides. Lay them flat and spoon the burrito mixture in the center and sprinkle the cheese over the top. Fold the bottom of the tortilla up over the meat-and-cheese mixture. Wrap the sides over the mixture and serve, accompanied by Mexican rice and refried beans.

6 servings

Steak Tartare

MONGOLIA

From the time of the Khans the Mongols have been big meat eaters. Today in many of the finer restaurants their famous Steak Tartare, ancestor of the hamburger, can still be found.

1½ pounds ground sirloin or
    ground tenderloin
½ tablespoon fresh ground
    black pepper
6 raw onion rings, large

6 raw egg yolks
2 teaspoons capers
6 anchovy fillets
6 lemon quarters
3 teaspoons fresh horseradish

The beef for this recipe needs to be ground as close to serving time as possible. Make sure that the meat is fresh and has been properly refrigerated. As a precaution against Salmonella bacteria, place the ground beef and the egg yolks in separate bowls in the freezer for 10 minutes before preparation. Add the black pepper to the ground beef and form into six small, round cakes. Make a depression in the center of each cake and place an onion ring around the depression forming a small collar. Place an egg yolk in the center of each depression, and top each yolk with a few capers. Garnish with anchovy fillets. Serve with the lemon quarters and horseradish, accompanied by toast and a salad.

6 servings

Ground Lamb Kebabs
(Kabab Masala)

PAKISTAN

Most people in this East Asian nation follow the dietary rules of Islam. Their meals are concocted to bring flavor and spices to whatever they prepare.

*1½ pounds ground lamb or
   ground beef*
½ teaspoon cumin
3 garlic cloves, chopped fine
1 teaspoon grated ginger
1 tablespoon lemon juice
1 medium onion, chopped
1 teaspoon salt

½ teaspoon turmeric
*3 tablespoons chopped fresh
   coriander*
6 wooden skewers
*1 tablespoon butter or margarine,
   melted*
Butter or nonstick cooking spray

In a large mixing bowl combine the ground meat, cumin, garlic, ginger, lemon juice, onion, salt, turmeric, and coriander. Mix thoroughly and set aside for 30 minutes. Preheat the oven broiler (or your charcoal grill for a more traditional taste). Coat the skewers with the melted butter or margarine. Pinch off a piece of the meat mixture and press around the skewer in an oblong shape. Put two or three on each skewer.

If cooking in an oven broiler, cover the broiling pan with aluminum foil and spray with cooking spray to prevent sticking. On a charcoal grill, coat the grill with butter or nonstick cooking spray. Broil for 5 minutes on each side or until brown. Serve hot with raw vegetables and plain yogurt for a traditional meal.

6 servings

Corn and Beef Soufflé
(Pastel de Choclo)

PERU

This Peruvian recipe combines Spanish influence and Incan cooking techniques.

BEEF MIXTURE

2 teaspoons vegetable oil
1 pound ground chuck or
   ground round
1 small green bell pepper, chopped
2 medium onions, chopped
1 garlic clove, chopped
2 medium tomatoes, chopped

$^1\!/_4$ cup raisins
1 teaspoon brown sugar
$^1\!/_4$ teaspoon ground black pepper
$^1\!/_2$ teaspoon marjoram
$^1\!/_4$ teaspoon salt
$^1\!/_2$ teaspoon cumin

CORN TOPPING

2 tablespoons flour
$^1\!/_4$ teaspoon salt
$^1\!/_2$ cup whole milk
1 8-ounce can whole kernel corn

3 large eggs, separated
$^1\!/_4$ cup chopped green olives
   with pimientos

For the beef mixture: Preheat oven to 350 degrees F. Put the vegetable oil in a large frying pan and heat over medium heat. Add the ground beef, bell pepper, onions, and garlic.

Cook until ground beef is browned and onions are soft. Add the tomatoes, raisins, sugar, black pepper, marjoram, salt, and cumin. Mix well and cook for 2 minutes more. Remove from the heat and pour the cooked mixture into a well-greased $2^1\!/_2$ quart casserole dish. Set aside.

141

For the corn topping: In a medium 2 quart saucepan combine the flour and salt and gently pour in the milk, stirring to blend. Add the corn and cook over medium heat until the mixture has thickened and starts to boil. Stir constantly and allow to boil for 1 minute. Add the egg yolks and blend in well. Allow mixture to boil and remove from heat. Allow it to cool. In a large mixing bowl whip the egg whites until they are stiff, but not yet dry. Fold the corn mixture and the chopped olives into the stiffened egg whites. Pour over the meat mixture in the casserole dish. Bake for 30 minutes. Test with a knife in the center. When the knife comes out clean it is done. Serve with rice and a salad.

6 to 8 servings

Ponchero Beef
(Poncherong Baka)

PHILIPPINES

This island nation situated in the Pacific ocean is a mixture of many cultures and peoples, and has developed a menu and food selection unlike anyone else's in the world.

6 cups of water
1½ pounds ground chuck
   or ground round
1 large potato, peeled, quartered
1 ripe plantain, sliced in ¼-inch
   slices
2 tablespoons vegetable oil
2 garlic cloves, crushed
4 ounces sliced pepperoni
   (or chorizo sausage for a more
   traditional flavor)

1 6-ounce can chickpeas
¼ pound green beans
½ head small cabbage, chopped
1 bunch scallions
1 small onion, quartered
¼ teaspoon salt
8 peppercorns

In a large saucepan combine the water and the ground beef. Boil the beef until tender. Remove from the broth and set aside. Add the potato to the broth and boil until cooked but not soft, about 5 to 7 minutes. Remove from the broth and set aside. Add the plantain to the broth and boil until cooked but not soft, about 2 to 3 minutes. Set aside.

Heat the vegetable oil in a large frying pan over medium heat. Add the garlic and brown. Add the beef, pepperoni (or chorizo), chickpeas, green beans, cabbage, and scallions. Pour in the meat broth and mix together well. Add the onion, salt, and peppercorns and allow to simmer until the vegetables are soft and cooked. Serve with rice.

6 servings

143

Beef Patties
(Kotlety Wolowe)

POLAND

The Poles have interacted with dozens of cultures throughout the centuries. We find their dishes a wonderful mixture from all of these cultures.

2 pounds ground chuck or
   ground round
2/3 cup dry bread crumbs
3/4 cup whole milk
1 large egg, beaten
1 medium onion, chopped fine

1/2 teaspoon mild paprika
1/2 teaspoon salt
1/2 teaspoon black pepper
1/4 teaspoon garlic powder
3 tablespoons vegetable oil

In a large mixing bowl combine the ground beef, 1/2 cup of the dry bread crumbs, milk, egg, onion, paprika, salt, pepper, and garlic powder. Mix together thoroughly and form into six patties. Press both sides of each patty into the remaining bread crumbs and set aside. In a large frying pan heat the oil over medium heat. When the oil is hot sauté the patties on both sides until they are browned and cooked to desired doneness. Serve with boiled cabbage and potato salad for a traditional meal.

6 servings

Carne é Plantain

PUERTO RICO

This beautiful island is a blend of old Spain and the Caribbean colonies. Puerto Rican cuisine combines simple foods and exotic tastes.

¼ cup vinegar
2 pounds ground chuck or
* ground round*
¼ teaspoon salt
¼ teaspoon black pepper
2 garlic cloves, crushed

1 cup of vegetable oil with a few
* drops of annatto*
2 large plantains, peeled and sliced
* ½ inch thick*
4 onions, cut in thin slivers

Pour vinegar over meat and add the salt, pepper, and garlic cloves. In a large frying pan heat the oil until it is hot and add the plantain slices; fry them until they are crisp and remove them from the oil. Sauté the onions in the oil until they are soft and remove them from the pan. Add the ground beef and cook until it is browned; reduce the heat to simmer and add the onions and plantains to the meat mixture. Cook slowly for 30 to 45 minutes, remove from pan and drain excess oil, and serve with rice and black beans.

6 servings

Hamburger Cakes
(Bitiki)

RUSSIA

The vast steppes of Russia and the diverse mix of populations and people have inspired many fine dishes, including this one.

1 cup fine dry bread crumbs
1/4 cup hot water
1 pound ground round or
    ground chuck
1 tablespoon dried, chopped onion
1/2 tablespoon salt
1/4 teaspoon ground black pepper

1/2 cup sour cream
2 tablespoons flour
1 tablespoon butter or margarine
3/4 cup condensed cream of
    mushroom soup
1 teaspoon lemon juice
1 teaspoon chopped parsley

Place the bread crumbs in a medium mixing bowl and sprinkle them with the hot water. Add the ground beef, onion, salt, black pepper, and 2 tablespoons of the sour cream. Mix together thoroughly, and pinch off enough meat to make a 2-inch ball. Roll the ball tightly, then flatten into a patty. Dust the patty with flour and set aside. Repeat with the remaining meat mixture until used up.

In a large frying pan melt the butter or margarine over medium heat. Add the patties and brown well on both sides. When the meat is cooked remove it from the frying pan and remove the frying pan from the burner to cool.

Add the cream of mushroom soup, the balance of the sour cream, and the lemon juice to the pan, and blend them well with the pan drippings. Add the patties to the mixture and sprinkle the parsley over the top. Cover and place back on the burner and heat over a low heat until the patties are thoroughly hot. Do not let the mixture boil. For a traditional meal serve with brown rice and red cabbage.

4 servings

Broiled Lamb Patties

SCOTLAND

Scotland is a land of poetry and Highland mist. Its people have resisted the influences of the Romans, Normans, Franks, and English for centuries. They developed a menu full of hearty fare to warm their stomachs against the cold North Sea winds.

1 pound ground lamb or ground beef	1/2 teaspoon salt
4 tablespoons green bell pepper, chopped	1/2 teaspoon Worcestershire sauce
1 1/2 tablespoons chopped onion	ground black pepper
1/2 cup cooked rice	1/2 cup bread crumbs
	6 bacon strips
	1/2 cup gravy

Place the ground lamb or beef in a medium frying pan over low heat. Cook the ground meat loosely, like chili meat, and drain the drippings to use for gravy after the meat is cooked. In a medium mixing bowl combine the drippings, cooked meat, green pepper, onion, rice, salt, Worcestershire sauce, and pepper. Shape the mixture into six round patties and roll them in the bread crumbs. Carefully wrap a strip of bacon around each patty and fasten with a toothpick. Broil until browned on both sides. Pour the gravy over the meat patties while they are broiling. For a traditional meal serve with mint jelly and wild rice.

6 servings

Enchiladas

SPAIN

Spain has done more to send its culture and recipes around the world than any other country. Their famous explorers carried with them recipes and cooking techniques that have influenced all of South America, the Caribbean, and parts of Africa.

2 tablespoons olive oil
1 pound ground round or
   ground chuck
1/4 cup chopped onion
1 teaspoon chili powder
1/2 teaspoon ground cumin

1/2 teaspoon salt
1/4 teaspoon black pepper
1 8-ounce can tomato sauce
6 corn tortillas
2 medium tomatoes, cut in wedges
Parsley for garnish

Heat the olive oil in a large frying pan over medium heat. Brown the ground beef and onions. When the meat has lost its red color and the onion is soft drain off the excess fat. Add the chili powder, cumin, salt, pepper, and tomato sauce and simmer for 20 minutes.

Fill the corn tortillas with the mixture and fold over edges. Top the meat with the tomato wedges and parsley.

Serve with a tomato-and-cucumber salad and Spanish rice.

6 servings

Beef Curry

SRI LANKA

Sri Lanka, once called Ceylon, has a variety of food utilizing the coconut and peanuts that grow so prolificly in its subtropical climate. Combine these ingredients with ground beef to make a novel and exciting hamburger.

2 tablespoons peanut oil	2 tablespoons tomato paste
1½ pounds ground round or ground chuck	¼ teaspoon cinnamon
	1 whole clove
2 medium onions, chopped	1 teaspoon curry powder
1 small bell pepper, chopped	1½ teaspoons salt
2½ cups water	1 teaspoon chili powder
¼ cup shredded coconut	½ teaspoon turmeric

Heat the peanut oil in a large frying pan over medium heat. Add the ground beef, onions, and bell pepper. Cook until the beef is browned. Drain off the excess fat and add the water, coconut, and tomato paste and mix well. Add the cinnamon, clove, curry powder, salt, chili powder, and turmeric, and bring the mixture to a boil. Reduce the heat and allow to simmer for 30 minutes, stirring frequently.

6 servings

Gingersnap Meatballs

TAHITI

When we think of tropical islands and exotic south seas tales we generally think of Tahiti. Their hamburgers, too, have an exotic island flair.

1 pound ground beef	2 tablespoons water
¾ cup dry bread crumbs	4 tablespoons butter or margarine
1 medium onion	2½ cups beef broth
2 teaspoons salt	½ cup brown sugar
¼ teaspoon ground black pepper	¾ cup gingersnap crumbs
6 teaspoons lemon juice	

In a medium mixing bowl combine the ground beef, bread crumbs, onion, salt, pepper, 3 teaspoons of the lemon juice, and water, and mix well. Pinch off pieces and roll into 1-inch balls. In a medium frying pan heat the butter or margarine over medium heat. Place the meatballs in the pan, brown them, remove them from the pan, and set aside. Add the beef broth and balance of the lemon juice to the pan drippings. Mix well and bring to a boil. Add the brown sugar and gingersnap crumbs. Mix well and return the meatballs to the pan. Cook covered for 10 minutes. Stir once and simmer for 5 additional minutes. Serve with fresh fruit salad and rice.

6 servings

Beef Noodles
(Guay Teow Nua)

THAILAND

This kingdom, where majestic elephants still walk the jungles, has managed to maintain a distinctive cooking style throughout history. Their particular use of spices with ground beef creates a hamburger like no other in the world.

1½ teaspoons cornstarch	1 small onion, sliced thin
¼ cup water	1 garlic clove, chopped
3 black mushrooms	2 cups broccoli, chopped
3 tablespoons peanut oil	1 teaspoon soy sauce
1 pound ground chuck or	1 teaspoon fish sauce (optional)
ground round	Salt and pepper to taste

In a small bowl mix the cornstarch and water into a paste and set aside. Clean and soak the mushrooms in hot water for 15 minutes. Cut into slices and set aside to drain. In a large frying pan add 2 tablespoons of the peanut oil and heat over high heat for 1 minute. Add the beef and cook until lightly browned. Remove from the frying pan and set it aside. Wash and dry the pan, place it back on the burner, and heat the remaining 1 tablespoon of peanut oil for 1 minute. Add the onion and garlic and cook until almost tender, stirring constantly. Add the broccoli and blend in with onion.

Add the cornstarch and mix with vegetables. Cover and cook for 2 additional minutes or until broccoli is almost tender. Add mushrooms, soy sauce, fish sauce if desired, and meat. Cook for an additional 2 minutes or until the meat is hot. Season with salt and pepper to taste. Serve right away—with white rice or rice noodles for a traditional meal.

6 servings

Ortaköy Burgers

TURKEY

From the time of the Great Ottoman empire to the present day, the Turks have followed a religious road in their lives and their diet. Here, traditional spices from this region make a memorable hamburger.

*1 pound ground chuck or
    ground round
1/2 pound ground lamb
1 teaspoon salt
1/2 teaspoon ground black pepper
1/4 teaspoon ground cumin
1 garlic clove, chopped*

*2 tablespoons chopped parsley
1 tablespoon olive oil
1 teaspoon oregano
1 teaspoon ground cinnamon
1 small red bell pepper, sliced thin
2 small tomatoes, sliced thin*

In a large mixing bowl combine the ground beef, ground lamb, salt, black pepper, cumin, garlic, parsley, olive oil, oregano, and cinnamon. Mix them together loosely. Form into six oblong patties. Grill or broil until brown on both sides. Top the burgers with the peppers and tomatoes and serve on a plate or a roll. Serve with couscous, tabouli, or rice.

6 servings

Ragout From Marosszek
(Marosszéki Heránytokány)

TRANSYLVANIA

Transylvania is generally associated with the fictional vampire Count Dracula. But the country has a long tradition of cooking that has helped influence many cultures around Europe. We have chosen a dish that, once you try it, is sure to broaden your conception of the country.

5 bacon strips	¹/₂ teaspoon chopped marjoram
1 medium onion, chopped	1 cup dry white wine
1 teaspoon hot Hungarian paprika	1 pound ground pork
¹/₂ cup water	1 tablespoon vegetable oil
1 pound ground round	1 cup chopped mushrooms
¹/₄ teaspoon salt	¹/₂ cup sour cream
¹/₄ teaspoon black pepper	1 tablespoon flour

In a frying pan over low heat cook the bacon, adding the onion and sautéing until the onion is soft. Do not overcook the bacon. Remove from the heat and add paprika and the water. Place over the heat again and add the beef, salt, pepper, marjoram, and ¹/₂ cup of the wine. Cover and cook for 20 minutes. Add the pork and the remainder of the wine, cook until the meat is nearly tender. In a separate pan, heat the oil and sauté the mushrooms for a few minutes, then pour them into the meat mixture.

Just before you serve the dish, mix the sour cream and the flour thoroughly and add to the finished mixture. Stir over low heat until well blended and thickened.

Serve with a green vegetable and boiled potatoes.

6 servings

153

Stir-Fried Beef with Green Beans
(Thit bo sao dau)

VIETNAM

Vietnamese civilization is almost as old as that of China. This land has seen many foreign influences over the centuries and has adapted many of them to its own cooking style. But the Vietnamese hamburger is the same today as it was centuries ago.

1 pound coarse ground round
   or ground chuck
3 tablespoons vegetable oil
1 garlic clove, chopped fine
1/4 teaspoon ground black pepper
1 teaspoon cornstarch

1 tablespoon sesame oil
1 small onion, sliced thin
2 cups canned green beans
1/4 cup chicken broth
1 teaspoon soy sauce

In a large mixing bowl combine the ground beef, 1 tablespoon of the vegetable oil, garlic, pepper, and cornstarch. Mix well and set aside for 30 minutes. Put the remaining vegetable oil in a large frying pan, and heat over high heat for a full minute. Add the ground beef mixture and stir until beef starts to brown. Remove from frying pan and set aside. Drain pan and place on burner over high heat. Add sesame oil and heat for about a minute. Add the onion and cook until almost tender. Add the green beans and mix together. Turn heat to low. Add chicken broth and cover.

Simmer the mixture for 3 to 4 minutes. Uncover and add soy sauce and cooked beef mixture. Cook over medium heat for an additional 2 minutes, stirring constantly to prevent burning, until the mixture is hot. Serve immediately, with white rice and fresh fruit for a traditional meal.

6 servings

Index

157

Index